GRAC
RESPONS ITY

GRACE AND RESPONSIBILITY

A WESLEYAN THEOLOGY FOR TODAY

John B. Cobb, Jr.

Abingdon Press
Nashville

Library of Congress Cataloging-in-Publication Data

Cobb, John B., 1927—
    Grace and responsibility: a Wesleyan theology for today / John B. Cobb, Jr.
        p.   cm.
    Includes bibliographical references and index.
    ISBN 0-687-00769-0 (alk. paper)
        1. Theology, Doctrinal.   2. United Methodist Church (U.S.)—Doctrines.   3. Methodist Church—Doctrines.   4. Wesley, John, 1703–1791.   I. Title.
    BX8331.2.C63   1995
    230'.7—dc20   95-1454

Contents

Preface

This book is one United Methodist's effort to come to terms with his theological heritage. It is not another scholarly book about Wesley's theology, although its discussions of what Wesley said are often dependent on the scholarly books of others. It does not claim to be the one form that the Wesleyan tradition could take today. In particular it does not claim to speak for Wesleyan traditions other than the United Methodist. I hope that some of what is said here can be useful for all Wesleyans, but this book approaches Wesley from the perspective of the problems and needs of United Methodism. It is a proposal for how this particular Wesleyan denomination can reclaim its past and move forward into its future.

Wesley's greatness lay in his ability to size up the situation of his time accurately and to shape a ministry that was amazingly effective in that situation. Perhaps to be faithful to Wesley would be to size up the situation of our time with equal accuracy and to structure our ministry in terms of this analysis. Since our situation is so different from Wesley's, it might be that very little that Wesley taught would be usable today.

This possibility must be taken seriously. Wesley's theology was formed with little awareness of the full implications of modern science—none at all of postmodern science. He was almost innocent of the epistemological questions that have preoccupied us for two centuries. He lacked the historical consciousness that is the presupposition of most contemporary theology. He had little understanding of aspects of human psychology that are now taken for granted. He did not anticipate the tidal wave of criticisms of Christianity in terms of its anti-Judaism, its patriarchal character, its Eurocentrism, its anthropocentrism, its colonialism, and so forth. He provides us no direct help in responding to the sexual revolution or the range of bio-ethical issues forced on us by the astonishing advances in medical technology. He could not have dreamed of a situation in which thinking of the end of the world would be realistic reflection about the threat posed by human actions rather than about a supernatural inbreaking of God.

To minimize the difference between our situation and his and to try to bring his theology over to our time little altered would not express our true relation to Wesley. Wesley's theology has served remarkably well to liberate Wesleyans to respond to changed situations as they have arisen. This has involved theological change, often quite drastic. To reject new formulations because they are not explicitly found in Wesley would itself be quite unWesleyan. But the history of our changes seems to have brought us to a dead end. After the decline of Boston Personalism, we United Methodists have lost our way theologically. We are fragmented in the extreme, although a certain ethos, derived from our Wesleyan heritage, enables the denomination as an institution to hold us together.

I prize this ethos. But without solid theological and missional underpinnings, the ethos fades. Our unity is fragile. There is danger that the United Methodist Church as an institution is becoming an end in itself rather than the instrument through which we share in God's mission in the world. Despite the enormous needs of that world, we have been unable or unwilling to describe God's mission in it in a way that would clarify our own role in that mission. Perhaps more serious for us as Wesleyans than the loss of a unifying theology is this loss of a unifying mission, but perhaps we cannot know what we should be doing until we know better who we are.

Many United Methodists call for a return to Wesley as a way out of our impasse. They sometimes remind us of how far we have gone toward realizing the fear that Wesley himself expressed in 1786 in his "Thoughts Upon Methodism":

> I am not afraid that the people called Methodists should ever cease to exist either in Europe or America. But I am afraid, lest they should only exist as a dead sect, having the form of religion without the power. And this undoubtedly will be the case, unless they hold fast both the doctrine, spirit, and discipline with which they first set out.[1]

Some interpret this as calling for a quite literal return to the doctrine and practices instituted by Wesley in a way that could have very conservative, if not reactionary, results. My own fear was that a "back to Wesley" movement would in this way lead to ignoring or minimizing the changes of the past two hundred years. This led me for some time to resist it and to expend my energies elsewhere. But I have found that most of those who call for a renewal of the study of Wesley do not suppose that Wesley's thought can be simply repeated today. Instead, they rightly believe that the movement he initiated needs to reappraise his work and the relevance of his thought for our time in order to find a shared basis on which to move forward. I have concluded that they are correct, and it is to that task that I hope to contribute.

The time for such efforts has come. Wesley scholarship has advanced greatly in the last generation due in large part to the leadership of Albert Outler and Frank Baker. One of the achievements has been to trace the development of Wesley's thought through his long life and ministry. It is now possible to distinguish especially three phases of his thought: the early phase from 1733 to 1738, the middle phase from 1738 to 1765, and the final phase from 1765 to 1791. I particularly commend here the work of Richard Heitzenrater and Randy Maddox. Although I have benefited from their writings, I have not taken part in this scholarly work or reproduced it extensively in this book. On the whole I have presented the Wesley of the middle and later phases.

The chief obstacle now to the appropriation of Wesley is that his way of thinking is, at least on the surface, strange to most of us. Our categories of thought are far less Biblical and far more secular. Even where they are Biblical they select in different ways from the Bible. Hence, initially, Wesley seems to be answering questions we are not asking. Chapter 1 is written for those many United Methodists who find "theology" in general an alien enterprise and therefore have no expectation that any theology, much less one developed in the eighteenth century, could help us now to answer the questions we are really asking. It suggests, selectively, that Wesley's answers to the questions of his day *can* help us to answer some of our questions. It also asserts that some of his answers require expansion and modification if they are to fulfil for us the role that they fulfilled for him.

One of the topics most central to Wesley was the relation of human responsibility to grace. He saw most of the views available at his time as either denying human responsibility in relation to salvation or else making people responsible for that salvation. He wanted to emphasize human responsibility, but only, emphatically, in the context of the primacy of grace. He could do this only by developing a distinctive anthropology, one in which God is constitutively present and active in all people. This anthropology is relevant to our dealing with other questions as well. Wesley extended the model to the whole of creation, and this contributes to needed changes in our views of animals and of the Earth. This is the topic of Chapter 2.

Chapter 3 shows that love is the central concept in Wesley's thinking both about God and about the Christian life. Its full meaning can only be understood in relation to the immanence of God in the world explained in Chapter 2. Not everything Wesley said about the Christian's love of God and neighbor worked well for him, nor can it all be used theologically today; but much is of permanent value. Wesley grounded this love in his own, unusual but fruitful, doctrine of faith, based on Hebrews 11 and his own epistemological theory. This, too, requires modification for our use.

Chapter 4 begins the discussion of what is often called "the order of salvation." Recent Wesleyan scholarship has proposed a shift to "the way of salvation" to indicate its processive character.[2] Wesley divides this into two parts, "justification" and "the new birth." Justification is God's pardon, and Wesley believes that not only are we objectively pardoned by God, based on the work of Jesus Christ, but also we are subjectively assured that this has occurred by the Holy Spirit. Hence, this chapter treats justification and assurance. Although his doctrine of assurance never attained full clarity and certainly cannot be adopted by us in any of his specific formulations, the concern for knowing God's forgiving work in our lives is important for us as well.

Chapter 5 continues the discussion of the way of salvation, dealing now with the new birth as the beginning of the process of internal transformation. Wesley called this process sanctification. He believed that it can lead to perfect love, which he also called entire sanctification. Wesley's honest account of the ups and downs of the Christian life, the possibility for real growth, and the continual danger of "falling from grace," are richly suggestive. Most controversial in his own time, and largely abandoned by United Methodism, was his doctrine that the process of growth could attain fulfillment in this life in entire sanctification. Wesley's general emphasis on growth in grace can make a lot of sense to us, and even his conviction that we should not set any limits to where this process can bring us is worth reconsideration.

Chapters 2 through 5 take their cues from central emphases of Wesley and consider the adaptations needed to make them relevant for us today. Chapters 6 through 8 focus more directly on questions posed by our current situation. But they, too, present Wesley's ideas in the process of answering these questions.

One of our problems today is that law and gospel have fallen apart. We rarely challenge ourselves by presenting high standards of personal living. Hence we rarely proclaim the "law" in an effective way. We do not want to make people feel guilty. In regard to personal life our effort is to reassure and comfort. On the other hand, some of us do contrast the society in which we live with the Realm of God. In this social sphere we do sometimes proclaim law. But we rarely connect this law to personal life. The issue of Chapter 6 is whether we can learn from Wesley how to relate law and gospel integrally.

A second question that concerns us today is how we can combine the spirit of openness that is so important a part of the ethos we prize with a clear sense of identity and enough commonality and unity to function effectively as a denomination. Our problem is certainly different from that which Wesley faced in creating a new movement, initially within the Church of England. Nevertheless, it is fruitful to examine how he related the spirit of tolerance and mutual apprecia-tion, which he strongly affirmed, to the disciplined unity of the Methodist movement. Chapter 7 treats this question. It considers also the appropriate relation of United Methodists to other religious traditions.

Since the Wesleyan tradition takes Christian life as its essential requirement, it is open to a wide range of theological thinking. The question of when that thinking is responsible is not answered by comparing its conclusions with a pre-established creed. But it re-mains important to have shared norms or principles by which to proceed. Today we have extracted from Wesley what Albert Outler taught us to call the quadrilateral. Chapter 8 examines the guidance Wesley gives us on the issues that now trouble the denomination, especially on the roles of scripture, reason, and experience, although tradition is also treated briefly. Of special importance to us is a question not directly addressed by Wesley: Do reason and experi-ence contribute directly to our theology, or is their function limited to the interpretation of scripture?

I would not have thought of writing this book had I not been invited to lecture to the Wesley Theological Society of Northern Illinois in February, 1993. Since I am not a Wesley scholar, I hesitated to accept the invitation. However, it became clear that their expecta-tion of me was to relate my own thought to Wesley, not to lecture extensively or with originality on Wesley himself. I gladly did this in a series entitled "Wesleyan Theology and Process Theology."

Re-reading some of Wesley in preparation for those lectures and appreciating the healthy theological climate that this twenty-year series had nurtured among the pastors present stimulated the thinking that has led to this book. I am grateful to the Society both for the invitation and for the conversations that took place. In this connection I owe a special debt to William Schweiker of the University of Chicago, who was my respondent.

The fact that process theology was thematized in those lectures and that my reading of Wesley no doubt involves a "process hermeneutic" should be acknowledged. Certainly I am writing this book, as all my books, as a process theologian. Furthermore, at certain points I explicitly make use of categories and analyses derived from process thought in interpreting Wesley or in proposing how his wisdom can best be appropriated today. Nevertheless, the book is not about process theology except as that is in fact one continuation of Wesley's influence.

I sent a draft of this manuscript to Rex Matthews both to test his interest in recommending it to Abingdon Press for publication and because I trusted his guidance as a Wesley scholar. He sent copies to several other scholars, and I am indebted to Kenneth Carder, Kenneth J. Collins, Randy Maddox, and Theodore Runyon for very helpful responses that have led to further reading and extensive revision and supplementation. Matthews himself was extraordinarily helpful, steering me away from several serious errors of both fact and interpretation and toward important literature that I was neglecting. Although I have given some indications in the text of what I have learned from these scholars, my debt is more pervasive than a few footnotes can indicate. It should not be necessary to say that none of them share responsibility for continuing errors in judgment and interpretation, especially where I have differed slightly from them. But I have no doubt that the treatment of Wesley is more faithful and reliable because they have shared their responses with me.

In dealing with a past figure, the problem of sexist language is inescapable. Obviously, Wesley used masculine language where we today strive to be gender neutral. I have not called attention to that with "[*sic*]." Outside of quotations I have avoided this practice.

Like Wesley's own writings, the purpose of the book is practical. Its goal is to support the struggle for sufficient unity in our denomination to enable it to function as a part of God's mission on Earth. As United Methodists we do not now have the unity we need in order to respond to God's call to mission. That unity must emerge out of the respectful interaction of the diverse groups who now make up our denomination. It cannot be found by simply returning to our origins.

On the other hand, unity cannot develop apart from our joint renewal of appreciation for our heritage. This book articulates elements of our heritage that may be able to guide our current quest for unity in diversity. Ideally, it is a proposal for so defining and strengthening our unity as to make of our diversity an enrichment instead of a threat to our shared future. It expresses my conviction that we can develop enough unity to act together effectively in a manner that is continuous with our distinctive tradition and faithful to our present calling.

CHAPTER 1

Making Connections

Where We Begin

If this were a book about Wesley's theology, it could plunge directly into the exposition of his thought. But it is not. Its aim is to find in dialogue with Wesley some central convictions around which United Methodists might be able to reach enough consensus to move faithfully into the future. It would not get us very far, therefore, if we agreed that Wesley did a good job of solving problems that were important in the eighteenth century unless we found that those were also our twentieth-century problems.

For example, we might come to appreciate the way Wesley related justification and sanctification. But for the great majority of United Methodists today this would seem initially to be a rather quaint historical achievement with little relation to life. To make this useful for our purposes, we would have to begin with some recognizable contemporary concerns and then show that Wesley's formulations relate to them in an illuminating way.

One difficulty in pursuing this task is that so many United Methodists do not seem to be asking theological questions with any urgency. Sociologically we are far more like the Church of England of Wesley's day than like the people who responded to Wesley's preaching. The mission to those people—the poor and marginalized—we have largely turned over to others.

We may hope, indeed, must hope, that if we renew ourselves in a truly Wesleyan theology, we will have a message of universal urgency: good news for all. With such a message we will return to a ministry to the poor and marginalized as well as to the affluent. But if our message is to be convincing to ourselves, we can only begin where we are. And if our message is not genuinely convincing to us, it will not be good news for others. Pressuring ourselves to "evangelize" when we do not know whether we have good news to share only digs us deeper into the pit of inauthenticity.

Until we uncover our own operative theology and pursue it, we cannot make authentic contact with traditional theology and learn from it. Nor can we formulate the gospel convincingly for ourselves. Where can we begin to become conscious of our real beliefs so that we can develop them and understand the theology of those for whom beliefs have been extemely important? I want to propose five points of contact as suggestive of the wide range of possibilities.

(1) We comfortable, mostly middle-class, largely secularized United Methodists usually become aware that we have theological questions only in times of crisis. When a child dies, or one's spouse leaves, or one loses a job, or one learns that one has inoperable cancer, one then asks, Why? And one is not asking for a merely scientific answer.

(2) Issues of public morality sometimes raise for us recognizably theological questions. Today abortion is doing so. Some are convinced that human life is "sacred." Believing that the fetus in its mother's womb is already human, they act passionately in its defense. Others believe with equal passion that women have the right to plan their families, to choose when and when not to bring children into the world. Both positions involve assumptions about the nature of human beings and the basis of their worth and their morality that connect with traditional theology.

(3) Fundamental convictions about what it means to be Christian come to the surface when a local church considers becoming a "reconciling congregation." Some find that to express their faith is to accept other people as they are. Others believe that to be a Christian is to live according to a righteous pattern. The former are not indifferent to righteousness, and they hope that as they include those who are openly gay and lesbian in the congregation, these will be helped to find a righteous way of living appropriate to their sexual orientation. The latter believe that the righteous pattern built into the nature of things excludes active expression of homosexual feelings. Neither position can be supported without making theological beliefs explicit.

(4) Increasing familiarity with other religious communities raises questions about established habits of mind within the church. Even those who are not engaged in a passionate quest for salvation are accustomed to thinking of Jesus as Lord and Savior. They have acknowledged him as such in their membership vows. When they have dealings with those who are actively religious, perhaps more

faithfully so than they themselves, but have no place for Jesus in their scheme of things, United Methodists are apt to wonder whether the claim of Jesus' importance is exaggerated. Some renew the conviction that it is not, that apart from Jesus there is no salvation. Others reject that conviction as an obstacle to mutual understanding and appreciation across religious lines. In either case they cannot avoid clarifying their Christology.

(5) Within and without the church the environmental crisis has raised theological questions. More and more people have recognized that traditional Western Christian teaching about human domination of the Earth has supported exploitative practices. Some move to recover a religious feeling for the Earth as "Mother" or "Gaia." Others identify that as idolatry but view the Earth sacramentally instead of instrumentally. Still others renew the understanding of human beings as stewards of the creation. Here, too, it is inevitable that theological convictions be articulated.

These examples indicate that even among relatively secularized, theologically complacent, middle-class United Methodists, theological issues do arise. Unfortunately, they are not issues on which we can turn directly to Wesley for help. The question of theodicy troubled him acutely with regard to the supposed election of many by God to eternal damnation. But with respect to the evils listed above, he had surprisingly little to say. It is hard to guess what position he would have taken on abortion. Sexual morality in general plays an astonishingly minor role in his treatment of the Christian life. Although he makes occasional comments about other religions, and discourages prejudice against them, his Christology is barely affected by this. He knew nothing of an approaching environmental crisis.

Nevertheless, at a deeper level there is a convergence between the issues raised in these current examples and those with which Wesley dealt. All of these issues raise in one way or another the question of how God is related to the world. This is a question with which Wesley wrestled extensively and brilliantly as it arose for him in reflection on the process of salvation.

(1) The questions "Why?" "Why did this happen to me?" take on religious depth because of a widespread, often scarcely acknowledged, belief in providence. Somehow people suppose that there *should* be justice in the ordering of things. As long as life goes reasonably well, this belief plays little role. But when evil strikes, the right order of things seems broken. Often the question is explicitly

theistic: "Why is God doing this to me?" "What have I done to deserve God's punishment?"

Underlying such questions is a view of God's power as controlling. Either it unilaterally determines everything that happens, or it overrules other causes with regard to important matters. This is a view that has strong support in the tradition, but much of modernity has rebelled against it. Secularism is to a large extent the affirmation that the causes of events are to be found in nature and history. In the deistic version, the laws governing the events are attributed to God. In the atheistic version there is no need for such an hypothesis. In either case God is not directly a factor in causal explanation.

In all of these major answers to the question "Why?" God is depicted as external to the world. The atheist denies the reality of this external deity. The deist affirms God as the cause of the whole system, who then lets the system run itself. The supernaturalistic theist teaches either that God directly runs everything or that God overrules natural causes from time to time. Today a widespread alternative view is a compromise between the deistic and theistic ones. It asserts with the theist that God has the power to control everything or to intervene, but it adds that, for the sake of human freedom, God chooses not to exercise this power. Thus it agrees with the deist that in fact God leaves the world to the operation of natural and historical causality.

It seems that if God is outside the world, the only way that events can be affected by God is for them to be unilaterally determined. The range of options changes when emphasis is placed on divine immanence. God can then be seen to be a factor in the explanation of events without being the sole cause of what happens. Wesley explored this alternative in ways that have still not been fully appreciated.

(2) The second example above dealt with abortion. The debate tends to be couched in terms of absolutes: the absolute right of the fetus to live versus the absolute right of the woman to decide. Such absoluteness is clearly religious, and the former right is often expressed in explicitly religious terms: Human life is said to be "sacred."

The form of the debate shows how far we have all come in the direction of humanism. Although Christians on both sides of the debate often appeal to the Bible and make reference to God, it is human beings and their "rights" that stand at the center. As belief in God has been displaced from centrality, it has become instrumental to humanistic concerns. The assertion that human life is "sacred" makes this shift explicit. Although many seem to think this is a Biblical doctrine, it clearly is not.

The Bible teaches that we are children of God, that God loves us and cares for us, and that we should love one another. Certainly, we should not murder one another! But this is not because we are sacred. Only God is sacred. True, we are made in God's image, but even before the fall, Adam is not sacred. Such language can only be applied to the Creator. We are made of the dust of the earth and return thereto.

Wesley focuses his preaching and teaching on the process of human salvation. This process leads to holiness. God is present and active in this process. Indeed, God is present and active in the entire creation. If Wesley had dealt with abortion, it would have been in this more Biblical context. Perhaps we can learn from Wesley new and better ways of thinking about issues of this sort.

(3) Today we are preoccupied with issues of sexuality. We have reversed positions from the view that sexuality is a necessary evil to the expectation that it contributes to salvation. Indeed, as a culture we seek salvation through sex more than through God. We are more likely to interpret religious practices as expressions of sexual desires than to locate our sexuality in a theocentric context.

When sexuality was viewed as a necessary evil, celibacy was understood to be the higher calling. This was true whether one was heterosexually or homosexually inclined. Now that our culture sees sexual fulfilment as a crucial ingredient in the healthy and happy life to which all should aspire, celibacy has lost its appeal. United Methodists on the whole share this attitude. Today most Methodists view celibacy as an inferior rather than a superior state. Yet those who are homosexually inclined are still required by official church teaching to choose this inferior condition. The result is a double teaching, first, that sexual fulfilment is a crucial ingredient in the life affirmed as good and, second, that those who are homosexually inclined are excluded from it.

Probably the strongest defense of this official position of the United Methodist Church is based on an understanding of creation. Heterosexual relations are built into the creation. God made humanity male and female. Male and female complement one another not only in bringing children into the world but also in caring for them and for one another. Sexual relations are a healthy and fulfilling part

19

of this mutuality. But separated from this mutuality they have no part in God's purposes. The righteousness to which Christians are called conforms to God's purposes as revealed in this created order.

The opposing view is that the current teaching of the church is cruel, that it puts law above love, that it suggests that human beings are created for "the Sabbath" rather than "the Sabbath" for them. For those who want the church to change its position and its practice, the appeal is to the Spirit's current teaching of what love requires rather than to an original created order.

Although Wesley does not discuss this question, it is instructive to see how he develops his ethical teaching for Christians. He does not altogether exclude appeals to natural law and reason and the Ten Commandments. But his overwhelming emphasis is on the Sermon on the Mount. A Wesleyan judgment on homosexual practice would need to be based primarily on this.

(4) The issue of how to understand Jesus Christ in the context of a plurality of great religious traditions has been important for theology for two centuries. Schleiermacher was the first major theologian to set his whole theology in this context. Today this pluralistic context is a commonplace of theology. Many solutions to the problem of "Christian uniqueness" have been advanced.

The point here is only to indicate that the different solutions to the Christological question often express diverse ways of thinking of how God is related to the world. If God is seen as essentially transcendent of the world, imposing requirements for salvation from without, and then entering the world supernaturally, in order to make salvation possible, there is little reason to adjust thinking about Christ in light of contact with other religious traditions. We must conform to what the transcendent God has revealed to us. On the other hand, if we follow Wesley in affirming that God as Holy Spirit works everywhere within the world for human salvation, then we are likely to understand other religious traditions as also products of that work. The question of how God's work in Judaism and in Jesus relates to God's work in Hinduism and Buddhism, for example, then becomes a theologically significant one.

(5) Although it is possible to treat the separate elements of the environmental crisis in purely practical ways, many environmentalists, even those not generally interested in religious ideas, have come to the conclusion that it is most fundamentally a religious crisis.[1] Human beings will continue to exploit the Earth in unsustainable

ways unless they come to perceive it differently. As long as it appears chiefly in the guise of resources for human use, even concern that some of these resources be left for future generations will not save the Earth from continuing devastation.

As Christians realize both that they are part of the problem and also that a solution depends on them, the issue as to how to understand the Earth in relation to God becomes more and more urgent. They cannot deify the Earth; that would be idolatry. But should they think of God primarily as the external Creator and Ruler of the Earth or primarily as immanent within it? When they think of God primarily as transcendent Lord, their task is to discern God's will as objectively revealed to them. To whatever extent Wesleyans follow Wesley in seeing God as working within the world, we will want to identify that work and consider how we can share in it.

Grace and Responsibility

Wesley may be regarded as the last of the great Reformers. For example, when Harry Emerson Fosdick edited *Great Voices of the Reformation*,[2] he began with John Wycliff and ended with John Wesley. This fits in several ways.

First, the Reformers were not simply thinkers, they were also organizers. The major branches of Protestantism today stem from their work. One of these major branches is Wesleyanism. It cannot be subsumed under the usual classification of movements from the earlier period of the Reformation: Lutheran, Calvinist/Reformed, Anglican, and Left Wing. Although Wesley was a devoted Anglican throughout his life, the Wesleyan movement has a different ethos, a different organization, and a different self-understanding from Anglicanism. Part of this difference derived from the influence of other branches of the Reformation, part from Wesley's distinctive appropriation of the Anglican interest in the early church, and part from Wesley's personal contribution.

Second, Wesley operated theologically within the same basic worldview as the earlier Reformers. Although he was aware of many scientific discoveries of which they could not have known, he did not see these as challenging the received worldview. He is the last major Christian theologian who did not experience a significant tension between the world of scripture and traditional Christian thinking, on the one side, and the new scientific worldview, on the

21

other. Already in his time other theologians were wrestling with this tension, and soon Kant, Hegel, and Schleiermacher initiated whole new styles of theology partly in order to escape the threat posed by modern scientific thinking.

This did not mean that Wesley was unaware of the major secular writers of his time and the directions in which they moved. On the contrary, he read widely. But he was not asking the questions they asked and hence found their answers farfetched or wrongheaded. Of Leibniz he wrote: "So poor a writer have I seldom read, either as to sentiments or temper."[3] Hume he described as "the most insolent despiser of truth and virtue that ever appeared in the world . . . an avowed enemy of God and man, and to all that is sacred and valuable upon earth."[4] He objected to Rousseau's "temper more than his judgment: he is a misanthrope; a cynic all over. So indeed is his brother infidel Voltaire; and wellnigh as great a coxcomb."[5] Mandeville he judged to be worse than Machiavelli.[6]

Third, Wesley was preoccupied with the same range of questions as were the earlier Reformers. He focused on the relation of faith and works, regeneration and justification, assurance and sanctification, law and gospel. But this does not mean that his doctrines repeated those of the earlier Reformers. On the contrary, they were quite distinct, and it was through their differences that they shaped the distinctive form of Protestantism that is Methodism.

No more than with the earlier Reformers did the focus on salvation mean lack of interest in classical questions about God, Christology, Trinity, and eschatology. These classical teachings were largely taken for granted both by the earlier Reformers and by Wesley, and they are presupposed in much that they wrote. These Reformers also made some contributions to the development of these doctrines on specific points. Nevertheless, current reflection on these issues is best carried on not with the Reformers but with their classical sources and in light of our radically changed worldview.[7]

What captured Wesley's attention and shaped his preaching was the account of how the saving power made possible and actual through Christ becomes effective in the lives of individual people. What is the experience of those who are justified and sanctified by this power? How should we preach and live so that more people can be saved? In short, what is our role, and what is God's, in the process of salvation? Few United Methodists today are existentially interested in pursuing these questions. Psychological categories have superseded theological ones in the common sense of the church. Yet in reality, even when we begin psychologically, without recognizing it, we come to the same puzzles with which Wesley wrestled.

Most United Methodists assume moral freedom and responsibility. The old issues of divine determinism and predestination play little role in their lives or thought. Yet when they realize that they have habits that are destroying their marriages or inhibiting success in their work, similar issues arise for them. Today they may define their problem as an addiction. The question is then whether they have the freedom to resolve the problem on their own or need help. Generally they are forced to acknowledge that their freedom does not extend this far. Indeed, until they admit their inability to deal with the problem on their own, they are unlikely to make progress.

Today the recognition that help is needed typically sends people to a psychotherapist or leads them to join a group. They assume that help comes from other people. But this is not unqualifiedly the case even among the most secularized. The psychotherapist may believe that there are healing forces working in all people, that her task is to help remove the obstacles that block these. She may even teach tactics or techniques that enable her clients to attune themselves to this growth-making power. Those who join a group for addicts often find that the reliance on "a higher power" is explicit. This is the case with Alcoholics Anonymous, the most longlasting and successful therapeutic organization. Members are strongly warned against supposing that they are capable of saving themselves or of ever supposing that they have grown past the need for help. The question of what role they can play in their own salvation is not always clear.

The theoretical argument about human freedom today is rarely couched in terms of God's grace. It is usually a question of whether the human condition, with its problems, is exclusively the result of some combination of heredity and environment. Most psychological theories are presented as if this were the case. But psychotherapists also know that when this view is internalized by the client, progress is likely to stop. It is important that the client assume some responsibility for the outcome of therapy. Yet it is difficult to incorporate this notion of responsibility into the explanatory theories of the science. Even if more emphasis is given to the healing forces within the body and the psyche, this situation is not changed. It seems that the outcome in each moment must be the result of all the forces that impinge upon it. Human freedom is hard to explain or affirm.

In this account, the issue of freedom has arisen in two senses. First, there is the question of whether people are free to save themselves from addictions or neuroses. One could answer this negatively, based on massive empirical evidence, without questioning that they are free to choose between eggs and cereal for breakfast. In relation to the history of theological debate, the former is the primary issue. It is the question of whether people are free to do what is truly good. Many theologians have said that human beings can make many choices, but that their motives in making them are always tainted. They do not have the power to remove that taint. Hence they are not free to do what is really good. Since the only freedom that seems truly important to them is this one, they declare that human beings are bound in sin.

Second, there is the question of ontological freedom. Are even the trivial choices, whose reality is not denied in the first instance, really free? Or, if we knew enough, would we see that they, too, are the outcome of our previous experience and the immediate environment? Many philosophers affirm the latter.

One can deny the first form of freedom and still affirm the second. There is a question whether the opposite position is possible. Can one deny ontological freedom and still affirm moral freedom? Philosophers who call themselves "soft determinists" often try to do so. Similarly, theologians who attribute all causality to God still want to hold human beings responsible for their sins. However, there is obvious difficulty in asserting that, although people's actions are determined for them by external agencies, they are still morally responsible. Too emphatic an affirmation of determinism, either natural or divine, is likely to weaken the sense of personal responsibility.

But what about denial of the first form of freedom, the freedom of people to do good or to participate in the process of their own healing or salvation? Does that weaken their sense of responsibility also? Wesley thought so. His struggle was both to assert the absolute dependence of human beings on help and also their ability to cooperate with that help. This does not seem so different from our present experience with psychological problems such as addiction.

Why, then, does the traditional theological discussion, including Wesley's, still seem so remote to most United Methodists? The reason may be that we make a sharp distinction between moral and psychological questions. We assume that in the sphere of morality we have free will. We assume that in fact we are quite capable of choosing the good. The traditional difficulty with this assertion seems to us perverse. It is only when we deal with psychological problems that the doubt about freedom arises. And on the whole, the tradition, including Wesley, neglected or ignored these problems.

As long as this separation of moral and psychological categories determines our theological reflection, we are unlikely to gain access to the positive contributions Wesley might make to us today. Hence, before working through Wesley's thought, we need critically to consider our own. Is our distinction of moral free will and psychological bondage tenable?

I suggest that it is not. First, the reality of free will is validly criticized by most of those philosophers who have examined it. It reflects a faculty psychology that has few defenders among psychologists. To support it on theological or religious grounds is to fail to understand the history of the discussion.

Second, the assumption that people can make morally good choices is usually based on a superficial view of morality. Let us assume that they can indeed choose to give money to a good cause or help someone to cross a street. Few have denied the possibility of good deeds in this sense. For Christians the question has been one of motive. If a boy scout helps someone across the street in order to earn a badge or advance in scouting, there is nothing evil in that. On the contrary, it is a socially constructive act of the sort that is essential to ongoing community. One goal of scouting is to build character, and that means good habits. All this is to be affirmed.

But are acts of this sort truly "good"? Does this orient the scout's life to God in an adequate and appropriate way? Does it reduce his self-preoccupation?

Usually Christians have thought that a truly good act is one that is motivated by disinterested love for God and neighbor. Is this something human beings can bring about by an act of will? Can they cause love to spring up within their own hearts?

When people examine their actions in this way, they see that the purity of motive that is required if they are to be truly good is as far beyond their capacities as breaking a well-established addiction. The gap between the moral and the psychological is reduced. This reduction also occurs from the other side. For example, psychologists are now talking about co-dependency. They point out that this is unhealthy. But this unhealthy pattern can no longer be compartmentalized as one problem which some people have and with which they need help. On the contrary, it seems that almost all serious relationships involve elements of co-dependency. In short, what is most valuable and necessary to a good life, loving relations with other people, is corrupted. Most of what have been thought of as virtuous actions in these relations are involved in this corruption.

Some critics believe that co-dependency theory has gone too far, that it implicitly holds up an ideal of autonomy that is itself not healthy, that some of what it declares corrupt is not so. Nevertheless, the basic point remains. We cannot separate psychological malfunctioning from the remainder of human life, leaving an untainted sphere for free moral choice.

I have emphasized the pervasiveness of our psychological ill-health in tainting the whole of our lives. It is equally important to include the element of moral responsibility in the psychological realm. Giving up simplistic notions of a free will need not lead to total determinism. The movement toward psychological health cannot take place without full personal involvement. People are as responsible in this realm as in any other. To understand all this requires hard thinking of a sort that is rare. Only when we engage in this thinking will we understand and appreciate the thought of Wesley.

Broadening "Salvation"

Wesley's whole thought and ministry were about salvation. Today United Methodists do not make much use of that word outside of ritual contexts. We know that our faith is supposed to "save" us, but from what we are to be saved, and to what, is far from clear. If we are to make contact with Wesley, we must either find some word that does name what we care deeply about or, better, reclaim this one for this purpose. Wesley can help us reclaim it.

The first obstacle to recovering "salvation" as the way to identify what is most important to us is its otherworldly connotation. For many centuries, what happened after death *was* of central concern to believers. The everlasting torments of Hell were a terrifying prospect to be avoided at all costs. Today we can no longer associate the Father of Jesus Christ with this understanding of punishment. Our focus of attention has become thisworldly. We trust our destiny beyond death to God's hands.

Furthermore, we now see that belief that what happens beyond death is supremely important has led at times to Christians doing, for the sake of otherworldly salvation, things that were harmful to people here and now. The extreme case was torturing the body for the sake of the soul. But far more pervasive was exploitation of people financially here and now based on promises of improved conditions beyond the grave. Luther was roused to protest because the Pope's money-raisers were promising reduced time in purgatory in exchange for payments to the church. Factory owners in Southern milltowns have brought in revivalists in order to discourage unionization. The list goes on and on, and Marx was not entirely wrong to call otherworldly religion "the opiate of the people." As long as "salvation" has this primarily otherworldly connotation, it cannot identify that for which we supremely hope.

But this does not, as we might suppose, separate us from Wesley. In this conviction of the importance of what happens in this life, we are all on the same side as Wesley. He did not understand salvation as otherworldly. Preaching on Ephesians 2:8, "Ye are saved through faith" (KJV), he wrote: "What is *salvation*? The salvation which is here spoken of is not what is frequently understood by that word, the going to heaven, eternal happiness. . . . It is not a blessing which lies on the other side of death, or (as we usually speak) in the other world. . . . It is a present thing, a blessing which, through the free mercy of God, ye are now in possession of."[8]

It was, therefore, salvation in this life that he discussed so fully. He, too, was quite prepared to entrust the hereafter to God. Certainly his whole theology and preaching presupposed the importance of our destiny beyond this life. But it is surprising how little most of his account of salvation would have to be changed if this context were dropped. His passion for salvation was not dependent upon it. Salvation here and now was the end for which he strove.

A second problem with the appropriation of "salvation" to name what we want is that it is largely restricted, in Protestant thinking, to the forgiveness of sins. In the Reformation, thought about salvation was concentrated on justification or pardon. The emphasis was on the fact that God's pardon is independent of any merit on our part and has no direct effect on our human, sinful condition. We today still desire to know that God does not hold our sins against us, and in this sense the mainstream Protestant understanding of salvation continues to have meaning for us. But if we understand salvation only in this way, then it can be only one aspect of what we care most deeply about, not the encompassing whole.

Wesley broadened salvation far beyond justification. He shared the Reformation doctrine that justification is by grace through faith, and at times he formulated this as a divine pardon quite objective to our experience. But he emphasized that in addition to *imputing* righteousness to us in justification, God *imparts* righteousness to us through sanctification. Most of his attention was given to the actual transformation of life that this imparted righteousness effects. Furthermore, this transformation is not only to righteousness; it is also to happiness. True religion, he states, "implies happiness as well as holiness." This happiness consists in "peace and joy in the Holy Ghost."[9]

Wesley's doctrine of salvation is thus much more inclusive of what is important to us than was that of the earlier Reformers. But its focus on righteousness, imputed and imparted, still omits much that we care deeply about. A girl dying of a curable disease may need to be pardoned for her childish wrongdoing and to become a morally better girl. But far more urgent is her need for healing. A woman whose whole experience has been distorted by childhood abuse may need to be forgiven of her sins and to become more righteous. But this is a secondary consideration. Far more important is the damage done to her and the need for repair. An alcoholic in many cases has sinned egregiously in the process of becoming an alcoholic. His guilt now drives him more deeply into drink. He does need forgiveness and actual righteousness. But even more he needs to be freed of addiction. A girl sold into prostitution by destitute parents also needs forgiveness and moral transformation, for undoubtedly she, too, has sinned. But it is far more urgent that she be freed from her slavery. The poor and oppressed in many lands may need forgiveness for their resentment of the rich oppressors or for their cooperation in their own oppression. They also need to live more righteous lives. But more fundamentally they need economic security and liberation from oppression.

If the salvation proclaimed by the church focuses only on the forgiveness of sins and the personal transformation that accompanies and follows from it, it has its place. But then "salvation" cannot be our one consuming concern. There are other things, omitted from the church's salvation, about which we also care very much. We will give some part of our commitment to the church that mediates forgiveness and sanctification, but we will give ourselves also to other institutions or programs that provide physical and psychological healing, and liberation from slavery, poverty, and oppression.

Wesley's emphasis on imparted righteousness is highly relevant to these concerns. The righteous will insure that the child gets medical care and that opportunities are provided for addicts and those who have been abused to get help. For Wesley righteousness requires the rich to cease exploiting the poor and the ending of all slavery. It certainly demands that the father not abuse his daughter! The poor are thus benefited by the sanctification of the rich; the daughter, by that of the father.

Although this brings Wesley's doctrine closer to our full range of concerns, it is still not adequate. Although for Wesley salvation has social consequences, the word is used in relation to personal transformation, not social. Despite the fact that Jesus spoke centrally about the Kingdom of God, Wesley does not understand that Jesus proclaimed a transformation of worldly existence generally. Wesley interprets the "Kingdom of God" to mean "true religion,"[10] which is religion of the heart. Hence the focus remains on the inner transformation of the individual that expresses itself in outward righteousness.

We now know that Wesley misunderstood what the "Kingdom of God" meant in Jesus' day. For us, as for him, it is important that Christians do good deeds and thereby reduce suffering and oppression, and we agree with Wesley that these should be motivated by love of God and neighbor. But for Jesus and for us, the Kingdom, or Realm, of God is a state of the world in which God's will is done universally—where all are healed and liberated as well as freed from sin. Accordingly, for us, all this is included in salvation. Does Wesley allow us to extend "salvation" to include healing and liberation? We will consider them in order.

Wesley did not think of salvation as directly including physical and psychological healing, but he came close. He thought that ministering to the sick is an essential expression of Christian love. This ministration includes medication. Furthermore, in the book he wrote to help the people with self-medication and good health practices, he stated that God does not will sickness, that it came into being through the fall. Restoring health is part of the work of renewing the normative human condition. It would be very easy to think of this as one aspect of salvation.[11]

In addition, the language he used to describe God's work of

salvation was often therapeutic. For him God is engaged in the cure of souls.[12] He was influenced by the Eastern Fathers for whom salvation was often interpreted as transformation from corruptibility to incorruptibility or mortality to immortality.

It would be a short step for Wesleyans today to recover the meaning embedded in the word salvation itself, wellness or wholeness, so as to understand God's saving work as including physical and psychological healing. This follows equally from Wesley's own preferred language of "holiness." We do not use that term much today, but its cognates, wholeness and health, are natural to us. Thus in various ways Wesley points us to an understanding of salvation that is inclusive of healing.

Another term, important to us and not directly provided by Wesley, is "liberation." Can Wesley's idea of salvation be expanded to include that also? There can be no doubt that Wesley affirmed the importance of liberating activity on the part of Christians, such as the freeing of slaves and the ending of economic exploitation. But did Wesley also affirm God as empowering the oppressed to throw off the yoke of the oppressor? Is this part of God's saving work in the world?

It would be going too far to say that Wesley directly taught this. His instructions to the poor to whom he preached did not include this note, however bitterly he attacked the rich for oppressing them. Nevertheless, Theodore Runyon has shown how much Wesley's anthropology and soteriology resemble and support that of liberation theologians.[13]

Runyon shows that Wesley's vision of the end toward which God works has remarkable resonance with liberation theology. He points out that Wesley's God "pours himself into the world to renew the creature after his image and the creation after his will. The 'design of the great Author' is that love 'shine forth in action' until all things in the created order are restored to their glorious state."[14] Wesley's own formulation is impressive:

> Suppose now the fulness of time to be come. . . . What a prospect is this! . . . Wars are ceased from the earth . . . no brother rising up against brother; no country or city divided against itself and tearing out its own bowels. . . . Here is no oppression to 'make (even) the wise man mad'; no extortion to 'grind the face of the poor'; no robbery or wrong; no rapine or injustice; for all are 'content with such things as they possess.' Thus 'righteousness and peace have

kissed each other;' . . . And with righteousness, or justice, mercy is also found. . . . And being filled with peace and joy in believing, and united in one body, by one Spirit, they all love as brethren, they are all of one heart, and of one soul. 'Neither saith any of them, that aught of the things which he possesseth is his own.' There is none among them that lacketh; for every man loveth his neighbour as himself.[15]

If we can affirm that God works toward this end, not only by imparting righteousness but also by awakening the will to justice on the part of the victims and to freedom on the part of the enslaved, then we can include liberation as an important aspect of salvation in a Wesleyan theology for our time.

There is a still deeper justification for expanding Wesley's understanding of salvation in these ways. This expansion is faithful to scripture, and nothing was more important to Wesley than such faithfulness. In the Jewish scriptures salvation is sought from all manner of concrete evils. In the gospels, too, God's saving work in Jesus Christ is depicted broadly. There are many stories in which Jesus forgives sins, but there are more in which he heals people of their physical diseases and casts out demons.

Furthermore, in Matthew's account, when John the Baptist sends disciples to inquire whether Jesus is the expected savior, Jesus points them to what is happening. "The blind receive their sight, the lame walk, the lepers are cleansed, the deaf hear, the dead are raised, and the poor have good news brought to them" (Matt 11:5). God's pardon of us for our sins is not featured in this demonstration of salvation.

Again, in Luke's account, when Jesus preached in Nazareth, announcing his salvific mission, he claimed to fulfil the prophesy of Isaiah: "The Spirit of the Lord is upon me, because he has anointed me to bring good news to the poor. He has sent me to proclaim release to the captives and recovery of sight to the blind, to let the oppressed go free, to proclaim the year of the Lord's favor" (Luke 4:18-19). Here, too, healing and liberation are central.

The gospels speak also of our lostness and our need to find the way. Nothing is more relevant to our situation today. Many Christians are truly bewildered as to what they should do in response to their personal, social, and global situations. Individually and collectively, in church and society, we have lost our way. This is partly because of our sin, but it is also because of ignorance, confusion, and the sheer pace of change. We are heading toward destruction and do not know how to stop or which way to turn. We need to reorient ourselves, or rather, to be reoriented; to find the Way, or rather, to be set upon it.

A minor note in the New Testament points to an additional aspect of what is supremely important for us today. "The whole creation has been groaning in labor pains" (Rom 8:22). Today human abuse of the natural environment threatens to make the world irreversibly less habitable, while people continue to increase their destructive activities as well as their own numbers. Humanity is heading for catastrophe. A Wesleyan theology for our time must encompass the salvation of the Earth as well as its human inhabitants. We should not expect to find this note struck clearly in Wesley. The threat to the planet that is now so palpable was not part of his experience. Nevertheless, the next chapter will note how Wesley did avoid restricting God's saving work entirely to human beings. For him, too, the whole world was involved.

No specification of the evils from which we need to be saved will be complete. Once we have opened up the meaning of "salvation" it can be filled in by all of us as new evils are identified. Today we know that we need to be saved from patriarchy and from racism. Runyon has shown that here, too, Wesley points in the right direction. But even if he had not done so, this would not matter. The basic shift is from a narrow view of salvation from sin to one that recovers the Biblical understanding of salvation from all evils. Then, as we spell out the particular evils that capture our attention at any given time, we will understand that the church witnesses to God's saving work to overcome them and calls us to participate in that work. There will no longer be a gap between what seems to us of greatest urgency and the salvation we proclaim in church.

Despite the intention of this book to be a Wesleyan theology for our time rather than an account of Wesley's own theology, it will not organize itself around the inclusive understanding of salvation for which it calls. This wider horizon will color much of the discussion, but most of its attention is directed to the topics to which Wesley addressed himself, and that means the content of the personal Christian life. If all of this were set in the context of affirming the whole gospel for the whole world, much of the detail would remain unaffected. This larger task remains an important one for United Methodists.

There is a third obstacle to recovering "salvation" as the name for all that we care most about. This will be meaningful in the context of the church only if we understand that God shares our concerns and is actively at work in effecting the healing, the liberation, the directing, and the renewal of the natural world, for which we hope. Many United Methodists today do not have the kind of understanding of God that makes this realistic or convincing. Here Wesley can be of great help. The recovery of his way of thinking of how God is in the world and what God is doing in the world can open us to the expansion of this thinking that is needed today. The next chapter, on "God and the World" will clarify how this can help.

CHAPTER 2

God and the World

Grace and Freedom: The Problem

A central feature of Christian theology from Paul to the twentieth century is the assertion that human beings cannot save themselves, that God is the only Savior. Furthermore, God does not save as a reward for virtue. God saves despite human sinfulness. Christians are saved by grace.

One reason for this emphasis has been Christian experience. Christian teaching, such as the Sermon on the Mount, has heightened understanding of how far people fall short or miss the mark. They know that they do not love God as God deserves to be loved or their neighbors as themselves. Yet they learn through Christ that they are loved and forgiven.

A second reason for this emphasis, noted by Paul, is that if one credits oneself for being saved, this leads to boasting or self-righteousness. For example, those who acknowledge that only because of God's act in Jesus Christ is salvation possible, may still believe that it has been offered to all with the sole condition that one respond to God with appropriate gratitude. Some refuse to make that response. Others make it. The offer of salvation is recognized as pure grace. But the human response determines who finally receives the salvation. Those who made this response could then boast of having done so. They have performed one righteous act that others failed to perform. It is finally because they are better persons that they are saved. Reaction to this reasoning has led to extreme measures in excluding human merit.

To exclude the possibility of boasting many theologians argue that not only the offer of salvation but also its acceptance is the work of God. It is the Holy Spirit who opens us to the gift, not the human will. Left to their own devices human beings would always oppose and reject. God overcomes this resistance. Hence salvation is purely the work of God.

But why does God overcome the resistance of some and not of others? Is it because the resistance of some is weaker? No, that would allow, once again, a space for boasting. Those who resist less would be the better persons, and this virtue, or lesser sin, would be the final reason for their salvation. To prevent this conclusion from being drawn, it is asserted that God saves whomever God will, with no regard whatsoever for their virtue.

This move has highly unattractive logical consequences. The first such consequence has to do with the character of God. If salvation is in no way conditioned by human response, then why does God not save all? Karl Barth saw the force of this objection and opted in the end for something very much like universal salvation. But in that case salvation has no apparent consequences in this life. It is even disconnected from faith. Prior to Barth, most of the theologians who insisted that God is the sole cause of salvation accepted as fact that only a small percentage of humanity was saved, that most are eternally damned. They asserted that, since all deserve damnation, there is no injustice in the damnation of most, whereas the salvation of a few displays God's unmerited mercy. They argued that, since God's choice or election is not conditioned on anything about actual people, it is determined from the beginning in the divine foreknowledge.

The second unattractive implication of this predestinarian doctrine is that there is nothing a human being can do. This can lead to fatalism or passivity. In the skillful hands of Calvin, this was avoided. One could argue that those who raised the question of whether they were saved with real concern showed that already God's grace was operative in them. They could be assured that they were safe in God's hands whatever doubts assailed them. They were shown how to live their lives in gratitude for God's gift. But the other logic of the doctrine has also found expression.

John Wesley was appalled by the doctrine of unconditional election on both points. For him, even more central to Christian faith than human sinfulness is divine love. He could not reconcile divine love with the belief that God created most people for eternal damnation. Equally, he wanted to call all to strive diligently to become holy. No one, he thought, could excuse indifference to this call by arguing that only the elect can enter into this path. Further, he found that the call for those who are justified to strive for sanctification could be equally undercut by the argument that the ultimate condition of human beings is settled without regard to their efforts. He was convinced that people would turn to holiness only if they understood that they had a responsibility to do so.

But Wesley did not adopt an extreme position on the other side. Quite the contrary. He allowed himself to be second to none in his insistence on human sinfulness and the total inability of fallen human beings to save themselves. Indeed, he went to great lengths in his conviction that apart from divine grace human beings are capable of no good whatsoever. He recognized how close these beliefs brought him to Calvinism. In "Minutes of Some Late Conversations" (August 1, 1745), he asked his famous question: "Wherein may we come to the very edge of Calvinism?" And he answered: "(1) In ascribing all good to the free grace of God. (2) In denying all natural free-will, and all power antecedent to grace. And, (3) In excluding all merit from man; even for what he has or does by the grace of God."[1] Elsewhere he argued that "the will of man is by nature free only to evil."[2]

Nevertheless, Wesley reserved his harshest polemic for the doctrine of predestination of some to damnation:

Shall this man, for not doing what he never could do, and for doing what he never could avoid, be sentenced to depart into everlasting fire, prepared for the devil and his angels: 'Yes, because it is the sovereign will of God.' Then 'you have either found a new God, or made one!' This is not the God of the Christians. Our God is just in all his ways; he reapeth not where he hath not strewed. He requireth only according to what he hath given; and where he hath given little, little is required. The glory of his justice is this, to 'reward every man according to his works.'[3]

He complained that predestination makes preaching vain, undercuts the motivation to good works, and conflicts with the plain teaching of scripture that God wills the salvation of all.[4] Whereas Luther and Calvin had seen in the doctrine of predestination grounds for assurance, Wesley saw the doctrine as undercutting assurance by leaving open for all the question of whether or not they were of the elect.[5]

It is not surprising that some historians, encountering these apparently conflicting emphases, exclude Wesley from consideration as a serious theologian. But this dismissal has been much too quick, and Wesley's own resolution of the tension has been insufficiently probed. Our question is now, How can Wesley agree so extensively with the predestinarian argument against human moral freedom, and then reject the conclusion that God arbitrarily decides whom to save?

The first step is his doctrine of "preventing" or prevenient grace. A human being can do nothing good, not even accept God's gift, apart from grace, but this grace is given to all. It works in all toward repentance and faith and sanctification. It is only because of this grace that there is any progress toward holiness.

Against Wesley it can be argued that if this grace works in all and only some come to faith, then the difference must be in the virtue of persons. Some cooperate better or resist less. This implies that human beings have some virtue apart from grace by which they can cooperate or reduce resistance. It is this virtue that finally determines who is saved. For this reason, according to these critics, Wesley could not consistently maintain that the human will is by nature free only to do evil. The possibility of boasting, they contend, is not excluded.

The critics have a valid point as long as the general view of human nature assumed by them remains unquestioned. According to this view there are self-contained human beings. One need not say that their existence is independent of grace, for their existence as such and whatever faculties they have are given them by their Creator. But saving grace, in this view, comes to them as an additional gift of God—from without. Human nature is the nature of these self-contained human beings. If this nature is incapable of any good, then it is incapable of a positive response to God's offer of faith. If the person comes to faith, this must be by an act of God alone.

Wesley understood this, and he explicitly rejected this view of human beings and of human nature. After reaffirming that one cannot make the least motion toward spiritual life on one's own, Wesley continued as follows: "Yet this is no excuse for those who continue in sin, and lay the blame upon their Maker, by saying, 'It is God only that must quicken us; for we cannot quicken our own souls.' For allowing that all the souls of men are dead in sin by *nature*, this excuses none, seeing there is no man that is in a state of mere nature."[6] "No man living is without some preventing grace, and every degree of grace is a degree of life."[7] Although there is no natural free will, "every man has a measure of free-will restored to him by grace."[8]

This last formulation has had unfortunate consequences in the interpretation of Wesley. It has been read to mean that human nature has had a faculty restored to it that was lost in the fall. This led many

Methodists to adopt a doctrine of natural free-will that is alien to Wesley.[9] This is not Wesley's meaning. Instead, the person in whom grace operates, by virtue of that grace, has some freedom to choose rightly. A measure of free-will is restored to the person, not to human nature.

Wesley made an analogous point more explicitly with respect to "conscience." Many writers of his time thought of conscience as a faculty introduced into human nature by God. Wesley agrees that it is found in everyone and that it is a gift of God. But it is not a faculty that becomes part of human nature. "No man living is entirely destitute of what is vulgarly called 'natural conscience.' But this is not natural: It is more properly termed, 'preventing grace.'"[10] That is, it is God's gracious activity within human persons that enables them to distinguish right from wrong and draws them to the right. It is similarly God's gracious activity within them that makes right choice possible and sometimes actual. Human freedom, human capacity to distinguish right from wrong, and human ability to choose the right, are all the immediate working of grace within the human person. They are not faculties restored to human nature.

Critics of Wesley can ask whether this move on his part has really helped his case or only pushed the question back further. Suppose that actual human beings are constituted of two parts: nature and grace. The question still remains as to how these are related. If the nature is wholly evil, then grace can bring faith only by overcoming nature. Nature cannot cooperate in the process of being overcome. The decision is still entirely with God. If, on the other hand, the nature is held to be able to resist grace—or not to do so—then the denial to nature of any freedom to do good must be abandoned.

This line of criticism reflects misunderstanding of Wesley's intention or else the denial that his intention can be coherently fulfilled. He did not think of actual human beings as composed of two mutually external and separable entities. The actual human being is an embodiment of human nature more or less enriched and transformed by grace. There are not two decisions, one made by nature and another made by grace, but the one decision of the one human being in whom grace is more or less effective. Without that grace, there could not even be a decision, but the presence of grace does not ensure that the decision will be good. How effective grace is at any time is partly a function of past decisions and partly of the present one. None of these decisions is made by a human nature deprived of grace. Therefore, the question of whether that human nature has some virtue enabling it to choose well does not arise.

The decision is not, then, a decision of human nature to resist or not to resist grace. It is always a decision of the actual person. To whatever extent that decision is to resist grace, to fall short of what grace would bring about, the reason is the continuing power of sinful human nature—and this is very great. To whatever extent it is to let grace do its work, this expresses the power of grace. The person experiences this grace as God's salvific work within, overcoming the power of human nature. The person as person cooperates with the grace because of the grace that is part of that person's being. It is not sinful human nature that cooperates.

Wesley is clear that grace is not a substance or entity introduced into human beings. It is the power for good. This power is not "given all at once, as if they had a stock laid up for many years; but from moment to moment."[11] Furthermore, this power is not a thing at all. It is the Holy Spirit, which is the life of God within human beings. That means that concrete human beings are constituted in part by the presence of God within them. Human beings do not first exist in separation from God and then come into relation with God. Their very life is already God's presence within them. They exist by virtue of their inclusion of the divine life within them.

In one sense, then, we human beings have much of which to boast. The relationship to God is constitutive of our being. God is present within us. But that also means that apart from God we are nothing. Wesley denied any merit to human beings, even for what they do by God's grace. Because Christians recognize that all the good they do is God's working in and through them, they rejoice and are grateful, they do not boast. Whatever theoretical possibility for boasting a critic may find, Wesley was convinced that those who appropriate this view existentially will be grateful to God for the ability to know and to do the good not as a possession but as an ever-renewed gift.

For Wesley it was extremely important that attributing all good to the work of God within us not reduce the personal responsibility of those in whom God works. This point is made emphatically in his sermon on "The Great Privilege of Those that are Born of God":

> ... the life of God in the soul of a believer is ... the continual inspiration of God's Holy Spirit: God's breathing into the soul, and

the soul's breathing back what it first receives from God. . . . It plainly appears God does not continue to act upon the soul unless the soul re-acts upon God. . . . He will not continue to breathe into our soul unless our soul breathes toward him again. . . .[12]

This combination of emphases on the primacy of grace, the inability of human nature to do anything good, and the full responsibility of the human person to respond appropriately to God's gift and call are at the heart of Wesley's theology. They can be combined with remarkable consistency by understanding the free and responsible human person as partly constituted by God's inbreathing moment by moment. If the reader falls back into thinking of God's relation to the human person as external, and Wesley's language does not always remind us that this is a mistake, his distinctive contribution on this topic is clouded or lost.

Wesley's doctrine may also help with a present-day problem. Whereas in Wesley's day the problem was to maintain human responsibility without crediting human nature with any capacity for good, today the negative attitudes toward human nature in so much of Christian theology come into conflict with recognition of the importance of self-esteem. We have become aware that for many people the problem is not that they think of themselves more highly than they ought to think, but that they feel contempt for themselves. The traditional teaching of human depravity does not help to overcome this lack of self-esteem.

Wesley depicted each human person as loved by God, enlivened by God, and enlightened by God. Each is also called by God to grow in relationships both with God and with other people. Each is empowered to do so. Not to esteem oneself would be in violation of all of this. But there are no grounds for esteeming oneself as better than one's neighbors, or of taking credit for good actions as an autonomous being independent of God's grace. If God, in some respects, works in and through one with peculiar efficacy, one rejoices and praises God for that. One does not think of oneself as achieving something important in one's own power.

The Holy Spirit

The previous section treated chiefly of grace and of God's constitutive presence within each human person. Lycurgus M. Starkey, Jr. has particularly helped us to see the near identity for Wesley of

God's grace and the Holy Spirit.[13] Wesley himself made this quite explicit in "The Witness of Our Own Spirit":

> By 'the grace of God' is sometimes to be understood that free love, that unmerited mercy, by which I, a sinner, through the merits of Christ am now reconciled to God. But in this place it rather means that power of God the Holy Ghost which 'worketh in us both to will and to do of his good pleasure'. As soon as ever the grace of God (in the former sense, his pardoning love) is manifested to our soul, the grace of God (in the latter sense, the power of his Spirit) takes place therein. And now we can perform, through God, what to man was impossible. Now we can order our conversation aright. We can do all things in the light and power of that love, through Christ which strengtheneth us.[14]

The Holy Spirit *is* God's gracious presence in all people. All that has been said about grace in the preceding section can equally be said of the Holy Spirit. Wesley extended and enriched the doctrine of the Holy Spirit in ways that still have much to offer us. A brief review of how the Holy Spirit had generally been conceived in the earlier tradition will highlight his contribution.

In the early church the Holy Spirit was experienced as a powerful presence through which charismatic phenomena occurred. These included prophesy on the part of lay people in ways that could not be controlled by the institutional authorities. These latter increasingly sought to prevent irresponsible claims for direct inspiration. The struggle came to a head in the Montanist controversy, and Montanus was condemned by the church leadership.

As a result of the church's response to the threat to institutional authority posed by the Montanists, throughout the Medieval period the doctrine of the Holy Spirit was developed chiefly in relation to ecclesiastic authority. The official pronouncements of the church were now held to be inspired by the Spirit. The Spirit's role in the lives of ordinary believers was obscured.

The Reformers rejected this dominant position. They emphasized the role of the Holy Spirit in the inspiration of the scriptures. They also emphasized that the Bible takes on saving meaning for the hearer only as the same Spirit testifies in the hearer's heart to its truth. Thus the Spirit is the author of faith in response to the proclamation of the Word. This is an inward working of the Spirit in the believer. The Reformers move some distance toward understanding the actual life of Christians as constituted in part by this living presence of God within them.

Nevertheless, they did not develop this line of thought. Since there was little suggestion of the divine presence contributing to the life of human beings before justification, a serious affirmation of its partly constituting the life of the believer would have required notions of ontological discontinuity in human nature at the point of justification. There was little in Reformation theology to encourage that kind of thinking. Hence, although there is some rhetoric suggestive of the Spirit's constitutive presence in the believer, the dominant conceptuality is of the Spirit as an external agency which penetrates, at times, into the believer's life.

Further, as for the Medieval theologians, the primary focus in the doctrine of the Spirit was on authority. Against the Roman Catholics, the Reformers denied the authority of the church over scripture and hence the authorization of ecclesiastical pronouncements by the Spirit. Against the Spiritualists of their time, they denied that the Holy Spirit addresses new revelations to the believer. They held instead that the Spirit attests to the hearer the truth of what is revealed in the scriptures inspired by the Spirit. Since the Spirit does so by working faith, and since faith is the foundation of the entire Christian life, the Spirit pervades that life. But the Spirit pervades that life chiefly through faith; there is not an additional personal presence.

The association of the Spirit and authority characterized the Spiritualists as well. George Fox sought truth and guidance for personal life from the Spirit. Since the Spirit that had inspired the scriptures speaks in the same way today, the authority of scripture is in part superseded by the present working of the Spirit. This Spirit is the Light within, and this Light actually or potentially enlightens all. In that sense Fox has a doctrine of the divine presence as partly constituting human existence. But the Light is not the ordinary thought capacities of people. It is instead a point of contact with the supernatural world. It is more at the boundary of human existence than at its center. Even though the Spirit *is* a constitutive part of human existence, it is not hard to conceive human life in its absence.

The account in the preceding section of the divine presence in all human beings shows that for Wesley the major locus for reflection on the Spirit has shifted. Chapter 4 will discuss his interest in the Spirit as the source of assurance, but in this case it does not directly attest the truth of scripture. The major arguments for the authority of scripture are connected with miracles, the fulfillment of prophesies, the character of what is written, and the character of the writers.[15] The Holy Spirit attests to believers that they are children of God. Only indirectly is this a support for scriptural authority.

The major locus of attention to the Holy Spirit in Wesley was the question of how human beings are enabled to do good and be saved. The Holy Spirit is the informing, transforming, and empowering energy. In this process faith is central and critical, but it by no means exhausts the work of the Spirit. The awareness of right and wrong, the impulse to the right, the ability to act on that impulse—all these are the work of the Spirit. In the process of sanctification, which is grounded in faith, the Spirit's work is not mediated entirely by faith. The Spirit works directly in the heart of the believer. The Spirit is also the Spirit of Truth and hence all true understanding depends on the Spirit. Like Fox, Wesley believed that the Spirit is the Light that enlightens everyone coming into the world. But for Wesley this was the general light of ordinary understanding and reason rather than a special contact with supernatural information.

Understood in this way as the power that works for good and the light that guides toward truth, the Spirit is at the center of ordinary human life. Indeed, it virtually constitutes that life. Human existence as we know it is inconceivable apart from the power and light that are the working of the Spirit. They are fundamentally constitutive of what human beings are. Perhaps even this does not state Wesley's view strongly enough. In a letter to John Smith, he wrote, "I believe firmly, and that in the most literal sense, that 'without God we can do nothing'; that we cannot think, or speak, or move an hand or an eye without the concurrence of the divine energy; and that all our natural faculties are God's gifts, nor can the meanest be exerted without the assistance of His Spirit."[16]

In these ways Wesley's doctrine forces consideration of how God can be constitutive of human existence in a way that few earlier formulations have done. This expressed itself in his doctrine of the abstractness of human nature apart from grace. The actual human person is constituted in very fundamental ways by the presence and activity of the Holy Spirit.

Enthusiasm and Mysticism

In Wesley's day "enthusiasm" was a bad word. It retained something of its etymological meaning—being possessed by a god. Carried over into the Christian context, it referred to those Christians who believed that God was working and speaking directly in and to them. This could lead to holding that the present message from God superseded the Bible as authority for them. It could also lead to identifying ecstatic experience and activity closely with what the Holy Spirit effects and calls for in all. And it could lead individuals to act on disruptive impulses, supposing that these were the work of the Spirit.

In the twentieth century the Pentecostal movement has reintroduced "enthusiasm" in the sense of understanding the Holy Spirit as working immediately and speaking directly. It has tried to avoid the excesses that had led to the earlier hostile reaction, but it has not been entirely successful in doing so. The charismatic movement in the oldline churches is also an expression of "enthusiasm." The word "enthusiasm" has lost this specific meaning for us. It has become a quite positive word. We want people to be enthusiastic about their faith and their church. But the suspicion of Pentecostalism and the charismatic movement remain widespread.

In reaction to the threat of "enthusiasm," most theologians in Wesley's day carefully avoided language that suggested that God effected changes in us from within. Justification, for example, is something that God does to us from without. Any changes within Christians as a result of justification are explained as the consequence of knowledge or assurance that they are saved. They gain that assurance from reading the Bible or hearing it preached. The fruits of the Spirit are the changes in personal character effected in this indirect way.

The Reformers had affirmed that the Holy Spirit confirms to the believer the truth of the gospel message. The language often suggests an inward working. But in reaction to enthusiasm, the rhetoric of their followers became more careful to exclude that interpretation. The existential note was also weakened. The idea of subjective faith as the work of the Spirit within the believer could be avoided in two ways. First, faith could be understood as a reasonable belief that the gospel message is true, a belief requiring no supernatural source. This belief then makes the objective work of salvation effective in the believer. Alternately, predestination could be so emphasized that there is no need for any separate present work of the Spirit within in order to effect faith, justification, or anything else. When, in spite of this, faith was described as a gift of the Spirit distinct from justification, this was understood as coming from without.

Having been so careful to undercut "enthusiasm" by stressing the externality of God to human beings, theologians of Wesley's day rightly recognized that Wesley, in turn, undercut them. Wesley preached that God as the Holy Spirit is truly within us. To most theologians of the time that sounded like the "enthusiasm" they were at such pains to prevent. Accordingly, no charge against Wesley was more persistent than that he was an "enthusiast," or what we would today call a charismatic.

The charge was not entirely without justification. Wesley *did* affirm the immediate working of the Holy Spirit within human beings and that this working could be, and should be, felt. This comes out most clearly in his doctrine of assurance, but it is part of his whole understanding of grace. Furthermore, those who heard his message and believed often had ecstatic experiences.

It was very important to Wesley to deny the charge of "enthusiasm," but it was even more important to defend the Biblical understanding of the work of the Spirit within us. To succumb to the purely rationalistic and objective understanding of faith and justification was, for Wesley, to lose the heart of the gospel and the religion of the heart.

The importance to Wesley of differentiating his views from those of the enthusiasts was in part because the charge of "enthusiasm" damaged his movement and demeaned his theology. But it was also because there was a fundamental difference between his understanding of the presence and redemptive activity of God in human beings and that of the enthusiasts. For them, the Holy Spirit was something added to a natural human being whose existence did not depend upon the Spirit. The Spirit brought a supernatural dimension, typically expressed in new knowledge, supernatural directions, and ecstatic phenomena. For Wesley, the Spirit was the principle of life itself, of all understanding, of what is called conscience, and of every impulse to good. There *may* be extraordinary phenomena resulting from the Spirit's presence, but they are not the characteristic marks of the Spirit's presence, and they more often result from other causes. Expecting them misdirects attention away from the true Spirit.

In short, the "enthusiasts" began with the same view of God and humanity as did their opponents, that is, the externality of God to ordinary human existence. The difference was only that they believed that this ordinarily external God could also enter into and even take possession of a human life. Wesley rejected this prior assumption of both the enthusiasts and their enemies. God does not enter a person from without and take possession because God is already, always, a constitutive part of the person.

Whereas Wesley throughout his life shared the common rejection of enthusiasm, he had a much closer relation to the other form of religious life that is associated with finding God within. That is mysticism. Wesley studied mystical writings intensely during his early years; and it can be said that, in a very broad sense, he was a mystic throughout his career.

We can distinguish three phases of his relation to mysticism. In 1725 Wesley experienced a conversion to the conviction that the inner, spiritual life is of supreme importance. He immersed himself in spiritual literature, and most of this was mystical or quasi-mystical. Although this never meant for him any repudiation of nonmystical aspects of Christianity, such as the importance of good works, participation in the sacraments, or the saving work of Jesus Christ, mystical writings largely shaped his personal religious quest. Among his personal acquaintances he was especially influenced by William Law, who functioned somewhat as a spiritual guide.

His experience in Georgia and especially on his trip back to England led to keen disappointment with mysticism. He turned to the Moravians, who centered their inner religious life around Jesus Christ, instead of around the direct relation to God the Father. This culminated in his Aldersgate experience. At that point he was most keenly aware of the contrast between the mystical path that had so greatly influenced him before and justification by grace through faith in Jesus Christ. This led to severe criticism and even denunciation of mysticism.

The most direct and important expression of this attack on mysticism is to be found in his confrontation with his former mentor, William Law. He realized, at this point in his spiritual journey, that following Law had led him away from attention to Jesus Christ and especially his atoning work. On May 14, 1738, he wrote Law contrasting the demands of mystical discipline he had appropriated from Law with faith in the atoning work of Christ:

For two years (more especially) [I] have been preaching after the model of your two practical treatises. And all that heard have allowed that this law is great, wonderful, and holy. But no sooner did they attempt to follow it than they found it was too high for man, and that by doing the works of this law should no flesh living be justified.

To remedy this I exhorted them and stirred up myself, to pray earnestly for the grace of God, and to use all other means of obtaining that grace which the all-wise Godhead appointed. But still both they and I were only more convinced that this was a law whereby a man could not live, the law in our members continually warring against it, and bringing us into deeper captivity to the law of sin. . . .

But what is this to the living, justifying faith in the blood of Jesus? The faith that cleanseth from all sin, that gives us to have free access to the Father, to rejoice in hope of the glory of God, to have the love of God shed abroad in our hearts by the Holy Ghost which dwelleth in us; and the Spirit itself bearing witness with our spirit, that we are the children of God.[17]

The letter was personally critical of Law and elicited from Law a much longer defense. Law insisted that he, too, and such writings as *Theologica Germanica*, which he had recommended to Wesley, were Christocentric. Wesley did not deny that, but in his second letter[18] he did deny that either Law or the books he recommended taught the necessity of faith in Christ's atoning work.

From Wesley's point of view at that time Law's failure to highlight the importance of faith in Christ's atoning work either meant that Law did not appreciate its importance or that he mistakenly believed that Wesley already had this foundational faith. Despite his harsh tone, he did not reject the value of Law's teaching *for the believer*. This helps explain how he could and did continue to appeal to Law's writings as guides to the Christian life.

Wesley's opposition to mysticism expressed itself next in his break with the Moravians. Their mysticism was a Christ-mysticism rather than centering in the Father. But it had quietistic tendencies that now disturbed Wesley.

Subsequently, he came to a more balanced view of the mystics. He was able to appreciate a great deal about those he had been reading, and he wanted to share much of this with the Methodist people. But he now incorporated the contributions of the mystics in a context shaped by the evangelical message of justification by grace through faith alone. He distinguished the "gold" in the mystical writings from the "dross." For example, in 1776 he published extracts from Madame Guyon, saying in the preface, "Yet with all this dross how much pure gold is mixed! So did God wink at involuntary ignorance! What a depth of religion did she enjoy."[19]

By far the most careful analysis of Wesley's relation to mysticism is found in *Mysticism in the Wesleyan Tradition* by Robert G. Tuttle, Jr. He examines systematically the elements in the mystical tradition retained and affirmed by Wesley and those that are excluded and condemned. Tuttle identifies five central features in the mysticism encountered by Wesley: "(1) awakening, (2) purgation, (3) illumination, (4) the dark night of the soul, and (5) union with God."[20] Although the mature Wesley did not emphasize this mystical language, he did not quarrel with the first three points. His objection focused on the fourth. He came to the conclusion that this dark night is not the will of God for anyone. It results from human efforts to attain union with God apart from the acceptance of the saving work of Jesus Christ.

Tuttle asserts that Wesley accepted the fifth feature of mysticism, union with God, and he points out that Wesley sometimes used this language.[21] This is correct insofar as such union meant "perfect love, centered wholly in God, and which no longer asks any reward for its good deeds."[22] Indeed, it was this goal that attracted Wesley to mysticism and caused him to continue to make use of mystical writings even after he had come to criticize them harshly. But insofar as union with God meant the annihilation of self, Wesley rejected this goal. He believed in the denial of self and freeing the self from all self-centered desires, but this did not entail the loss of personal selfhood.

Wesley's relation to mysticism can be summarized by listing first his agreements and then his disagreement. Wesley agreed with the mystics with regard to the importance of the inner life and its movement toward perfection. He agreed that this entailed attention to the springs of action rather than simply to external behavior. He agreed that the all-encompassing goal of the Christian life was perfection in love of God and neighbor, that this love inevitably and spontaneously expresses itself in service of others. He agreed that human beings could subjectively experience a right relation to God and not simply depend on the opinion that it existed.

Wesley faulted the mystics primarily for their tendency to view the development of Christian life in terms of human effort. They depicted the Christian life in terms of human beings contacting and enlarging the divine presence that was within them. They underestimated the depth of human sinfulness which prevents humanity, apart from divine initiative, from moving toward God. Wesley opposed to this the primacy of grace. For him the divine presence within us is redemptively active. Furthermore, God has done for us in Jesus Christ what no human beings can do for themselves, and all real progress in spiritual life depends on that.

Precisely because mystic teaching was so attractive, had indeed profoundly attracted him, Wesley sometimes spoke of it as demonic. More than any other set of ideas, the mystical ones have the power to lead believers astray. Hence mysticism had to be condemned. But for Wesley this did not in fact mean condemnation of individual mystics. This was not possible since many of them embodied so much of the love of God and neighbor that was for him the decisive test of genuine Christianity. In Tuttle's words, "If a mystic life manifested fruit that only faith could produce, even if the understanding of faith was incomplete, then faith, saving faith, was still evident."[23]

God's Presence in the World

The preceding sections have considered God's presence in human beings. This was Wesley's central concern. But for us it is important to consider how God is related to the world as a whole. Here there are far fewer passages on which to rely, and these, less central to his theology. Yet Wesley said enough so that we can be confident that he did not set human beings entirely apart from the remainder of creation. God's presence is not limited to humanity.

One of the clearest and most emphatic passages is found in the third sermon "Upon our Lord's Sermon on the Mount":

> God is in all things, and . . . we are to see the Creator in the glass of every creature; . . . we should use and look upon nothing as separate from God, which indeed is a kind of practical Atheism; but with a true magnificence of thought, survey heaven and earth and all that is therein as contained by God in the hollow of His hand, who by his intimate presence holds them all in being, who pervades and actuates the whole created frame, and is in a true sense the Soul of the universe.[24]

This is a remarkable passage. If it stood alone as the only place in which Wesley spoke of the immanence of God in created things, it would be unwise to make too much of it. But that is far from the case. The immanence of God in all human beings is a major and emphatic theme of Wesley. That this immanence extends to the whole of creation is the most natural and consistent view possible. That he expounded it here with such feeling shows that it is not a casual adjunct of his anthropology.

The contrast between Wesley's view and those we most commonly associate with the eighteenth century is remarkable. Descartes and Newton had depicted a machine-like universe. God was its maker, and like the maker of any machine, stood outside it. If God acted on it, it was by external causation. This picture was read back into the Bible and became the standard image in the minds of most Westerners for two hundred years. It is *that* God who has aroused so much incredulity and antipathy in the past century. Wesley's God, the Soul of the world, who pervades and actuates the whole of creation, and who enlivens, enlightens, and liberates all people, calling them to strive toward personal and social perfection, and empowering their efforts—that is a different matter.

It would be too much to expect that Wesley would understand the world in a way congenial to the new physics. That physics has taught us that there is no merely passive matter as the old physics supposed. Wesley was on this point a child of his time. He made a sharp distinction between living things that possessed a principle of activity within themselves and mere matter that has no such principle.

But God is immediately active in both. God "is the only agent in the material world; all matter being essentially dull and inactive, and moving only as it is moved by the finger of God. And He is the spring of action in every creature, visible and invisible, which could neither act nor exist, without the continual influx and agency of His almighty power...."[25] Apparently he envisioned a dual type of relation between God and the world. With respect to matter, which has no principle of motion of its own, God alone is the cause of what happens. With respect to living things, their capacity to move is itself due to the way in which God flows into them, thereby causing them to become agents. God is, therefore, not the unilateral actor in the animate world, as in inanimate matter. In the human instance the result is that most of what happens does not fully express God's purposes.

Wesley's dualism made sense in his time, but it does not fit with post-Newtonian physics. Still, the principle underlying his doctrine is applicable. Wherever there is a self-moving entity, God is present as the immediate source of that power of self-movement, moment by moment. But that power is exercised by the self-moving creature whose capacity for self-movement results from God's presence in it. Since contemporary physics shows that what once appeared as passive matter is in fact composed of energy events, Wesley's principle now applies to all of nature. Nowhere in the course of events does God function as sole cause.

This adjustment of Wesley's view of nature to conform to the primacy of energy in contemporary physics would lead to other changes in his formulations. Wesley understood divine sovereignty to be unilateral divine causation. Hence, in relation to the inanimate world, he taught that God is sovereign. This led him to extend God's unilateral causation to many factors concerning human life as well, insofar as much of this is determined by the movements of material things. He drew the line only where freedom and responsibility are involved.[26] Thus he could assign a vast realm to unilateral divine determinism.

If, on the other hand, we now understand that there is some principle of self-movement in all truly individual events, then the interactive character of the relation between God and creature, so brilliantly analyzed by Wesley in relation to grace and responsibility, can illumine the whole of the God-world relation. The primacy of divine causality is everywhere maintained, but the idea of absolute sovereignty, so disturbing to Wesley when applied to human salvation, can be set aside altogether.

I have proposed that with later developments in physics, Wesley would have given up his dualism. In any case, his dualism is quite different from the Cartesian one that has dominated the modern Western world. Cartesian dualism separates human beings from all the rest. Animals other than human beings belong to the mechanical world of matter. They have been treated accordingly by ethicists, economists, and many ordinary people. Christian protests have been rare indeed.

Indeed, to this day it is difficult to find Christian teaching about responsibility to animals. The World Council of Churches has spoken beautifully about the integrity of creation, but it has said nothing about the suffering human beings inflict on other animals. Only quite recently have a few denominations addressed the issue. Still very rare are sermons in local parishes that deal with the relation of people to other sentient creatures.

Wesley, like most Christian evangelists and theologians, gave his attention overwhelmingly to the salvation of human beings. There has long been a practical Christian dualism between humanity and the remainder of the creation, whose effects have supported those of Cartesian metaphysical dualism. The natural world, including its population of animals, is supposed to be good only because it provides benefits for human beings. But Wesley did not succumb to this anthropocentrism. He accurately noted that "the Lord saw that every distinct part of the universe was good. But when he saw everything he had made, all in connexion with each other, 'behold, it was very good.'"[27] Furthermore, God directs "all His power to the advantage of all His creatures."[28]

Thus Wesley affirmed the intrinsic value or goodness of all creatures individually as well as the added value of the ecological system that they jointly constititute. Together with the understanding that God is present and active in all for the sake of the wellbeing of all, Wesley's teaching provides a religious vision which, when genuinely appropriated, should re-form our way of relating to the remainder of creation. It calls for respect for all creatures, recognition of the importance of biodiversity and complex ecosystems, and working together with God for the benefit not only of human beings but of all other creatures as well.

Wesley's concern for other creatures is not to be affirmed only on the basis of the implications of his account of creation. He gave direct expression to it in other contexts. In his sermon on "The New Creation"[29] he speculated about what will happen to the heavens and the earth. He included specific attention to animals. As a result of Adam's fall these have been made subject to vanity. He associated this especially with death and predation, and showed real feeling for the suffering involved. In his vision of the consummation all this is reversed. Thus animals will share in the final salvation.

Although Wesley saw that animal suffering is inevitable in this fallen world, he also saw human behavior as adding immeasurably to it and as lacking the justification involved in animal predation:

What a dreadful difference is there between what they suffer from their fellow brutes and what they suffer from the tyrant, man! The lion, the tiger, the shark, give them pain from mere necessity, in order to prolong their own life; and put them out of their pain at once. But the human shark, without any such necessity, torments them of his free choice; and perhaps continues their lingering pain till after months or years death signs their release.[30]

For Wesley, God is far from indifferent to this suffering: "While 'the whole creation groaneth together' (whether men attend or not) their groans are not dispersed in idle air, but enter into the ears of him that made them."[31] And Wesley saw that treatment of animals is a matter of Christian morality. He hoped that these considerations might "encourage us to imitate him whose mercy is over all his works. They may soften our hearts towards the meaner creatures, knowing that the Lord careth for them."[32]

Peripheral as Wesley's concern for nonhuman animals was, it contrasts with the total silence we usually meet in theologians. According to Randy Maddox,

Wesley's anthropology recognized four basic human relationships: with God, with other humans, with lower animals, and with ourselves. A holy (and whole!) person is one in whom all of these relationships are properly expressed. The proper relationship to God is knowing, loving, obeying, and enjoying God eternally (i.e., participation!). The proper relationship to other humans is loving service. The proper relationship to all other animals is loving protection. When each of these relationships are properly expressed, we will also have a proper relationship to ourselves of self-acceptance.[33]

The passage with which this section began emphasizes God's active presence in all things. It also mentions that all things are "contained by God in the hollow of His hand." Thus, not only is God in all things, but all things are in God. This point is repeated elsewhere. It is closely related to the way Wesley interprets omnipresence as entailing omniscience. It is because God *is* everywhere that God knows all that is and occurs.[34] One way in which we are contained in God is in God's omniscience. "Nothing is distant to Him in whom we live and move and have our being."[35]

Wesley does not himself draw the implications of this view. In his treatment of love of neighbor, he does not show that it is through service of neighbor that one serves God. Yet the basis for such teaching is given here. If all things are in God, then what one does to one's neighbor one does to God also. God then quite literally rejoices with those who rejoice and weeps with those who weep. Since one's neighbors are not only the human ones but also all the creatures that make up God's world, there are grounds in Wesley for affirming the importance of that world and all the rich diversity within it. Wesleyans are among those who today are taking the lead in the affirmation, in the language of the World Council of Churches, of the integrity of creation.

CHAPTER 3

Love and Faith

The Centrality of Love

The word "love" does not stand out in Wesley's rhetoric as exceptionally prominent. He did not preach a series of sermons on love. The word appears in the title of only one of his major sermons: "God's Love for Fallen Men."[1] Wesley did not begin with a definition of love and then derive its consequences. He did not say that we should love God and then do what we please. Nevertheless, it would distort Wesley very little to present his whole theology around the one word, "love." God is love, and Wesley would say nothing of God that did not cohere with this claim. God's creation and governance of the world all express God's love for the creatures. Even more clearly, God's work for salvation in Jesus Christ and through the Holy Spirit embody a passionate love of human beings.

The new birth is the coming of love to dominance among human beings. This is the love of God and neighbor. The new birth is the beginning of the process of sanctification in which that love grows stronger and more dominant over other motives. This culminates in entire sanctification, in which human beings attain to perfect love. All other springs of action have disappeared, and love alone remains. Holiness is thus nothing other than love. This whole process is the love of God working in our hearts to bring forth human love.

There are many direct statements of Wesley confirming the centrality of love. Near the beginning of *An Earnest Appeal to Men of Reason and Religion* he described Christianity as follows: "this we conceive to be no other than love: the love of God and of all mankind; the loving God with all our heart and soul and strength, as having first loved *us*, as the fountain of all the good we have received, and of all we ever hope to enjoy; and the loving every soul which God hath made, every man on earth, as our own soul."[2] And in "A Plain Account of Genuine Christianity," in answer to the question, Who is a Christian? he wrote:

Above all remembering that God is love, he is conformed to the same likeness. He is full of love to his neighbour; of universal love, not confined to one sect or party, not restrained to those who agree with him in opinions, or in outward modes of worship, or to those who are allied to him by blood or recommended by nearness of place. . . . But his love resembles that of him whose mercy is over all his works.[3]

Rhetorically, the centrality of divine love comes to expression most powerfully in the hymns of early Methodism. A hymn by John Wesley's brother, Charles, expresses their shared vision and has played a significant role in shaping the sensibility of United Methodism. Familiar as it is, it is worthwhile to look at it closely:

> Love divine, all loves excelling,
>   Joy of heaven, to earth come down,
> Fix in us thy humble dwelling,
>   All thy faithful mercies crown!
> Jesus, thou art all compassion,
>   Pure, unbounded love thou art;
> Visit us with thy salvation!
>   Enter every trembling heart.
>
> Come, almighty to deliver,
>   Let us all thy grace receive;
> Suddenly return, and never,
>   Never more thy temples leave.
> Thee we would be always blessing,
>   Serve thee as thy hosts above,
> Pray, and praise thee without ceasing,
>   Glory in thy perfect love.
>
> Finish then thy new creation,
>   Pure and spotless let us be;
> Let us see thy great salvation
>   Perfectly restored in thee;
> Changed from glory into glory,
>   Till in heaven we take our place,
> Till we cast our crowns before thee,
>   Lost in wonder, love, and praise.[4]

The hymn addresses God as "Love Divine." The whole hymn follows from understanding God as Love that pours itself into human beings. Everything said about God is adjusted to this starting point. Since the main issue in Wesley's day was to relate this understanding of God as Love Divine to the idea of God's omnipotent sovereignty, it is of interest to note here the appearance of "almighty" in the second verse. Many prayers and hymns address God as "The Almighty" rather than as Love Divine. The Wesleys did not avoid the language of divine power, but they were careful about unqualified use of power rhetoric, or allowing that rhetoric to shape the discourse as a whole.

In this case, the second verse is sometimes sung as if "almighty" were a way of addressing God, as if it were written, "Come, Almighty, to deliver." This reading is encouraged by the capitalization of "Almighty" in *The United Methodist Hymnal*, although, fortunately, the editors refrained from placing a comma after it.[5] But addressing God simply as "Almighty" would not be Wesleyan. In this context it would be asking the Omnipotent One to take one form of action, namely, deliverance, when divine power might be used in other ways. The Wesleys did not think of divine power in this abstract sense. It is power to create, to govern, and to save, and all these are acts of Divine Love. Indeed, they tell us what Divine Love is. Hence, in this hymn, Divine Love is characterized as "almighty to deliver." Divine Love is the only power there is for deliverance.

The focus in this hymn is on God's love of us and our dependence on that love's indwelling us. In regard to the effects in our life, the word "love" does not appear until the final line of the last verse. But this does not mean that the human response to Love Divine is something other than love. In the second verse the effects identified are always blessing, serving, praying to, praising, and glorying in God. In the final verse, human love is associated with wonder and praise in the culminating human response to Love Divine.

That love defines the Christian life is brought out with special force by Wesley's famous sermon, "The Almost Christian."[6] In this sermon he described himself as he was before his Aldersgate experience. He obeyed the Golden Rule, but he went far beyond that. Describing himself in the third person, he wrote:

> In doing good he does not confine himself to cheap and easy offices of kindness, but labours and suffers for the profit of many, that by all means he may help some. In spite of toil or pain, 'whatsoever his hand findeth to do, he doth it with his might,' whether it be for his friends or for his enemies, for the evil or for the good. For, being 'not slothful in' this or in any 'business,' as he hath opportunity he

59

doth 'good,' all manner of good, 'to all men,' and to their souls as well as their bodies.[7]

Wesley went on to describe his efforts to bring others to Christ, his faithful and serious participation in the life of the church, his diligence in prayer. Furthermore, in all this he was sincere. "By sincerity I mean a real, inward principle of religion from whence these outward actions flow."[8] This is "a real design to serve God, a hearty desire to do his will. It is necessarily implied that a man have a sincere view of pleasing God in all things: in all his conversation, in all his actions; in all he does or leaves undone."[9]

This crescendo leads up to the question: What more is involved in being altogether a Christian? Wesley's answer was straightforward:

> First, the love of God. For thus saith his Word: 'Thou shalt love the Lord thy God with all thy heart, and with all thy soul, and with all thy mind, and with all thy strength.' Such a love of God is this as engrosses the whole heart, as takes up all the affections, as fills the entire capacity of the soul, and employs the utmost extent of all its faculties. He that thus loves the Lord his God, his spirit continually 'rejoiceth in God his Saviour.' 'His delight is in the Lord,' *his* Lord and his all, to whom 'in everything he giveth thanks.' All *his* 'desire is unto God, and to the remembrance of his name.' . . . Indeed, what can he desire beside God? Not the world, or the things of the world. For he is 'crucified to the world, and the world crucified to him.' He is crucified to the desire of the flesh, the desire of the eye, and the pride of life.[10]

He then added the second requirement. This is

> . . . the love of our neighbour. For thus said our Lord in the following words: 'Thou shalt love thy neighbour as thyself.' If any man ask, 'Who is my neighbour?' we reply, 'Every man in the world; every child of his who is "the Father of the spirits of all flesh".' Nor may we in any wise except our enemies, or the enemies of God and their own souls. But every Christian loveth these also as himself; yea, 'as Christ loved us.'[11]

To clarify what is involved in such love, Wesley appeals to 1 Corinthians 13.

Wesley added faith as a third requirement, recognizing that it can be separately considered, although "it cannot actually be separate from"[12] the love of God and neighbor. He hastened then to point out that faith is proven to be true faith by its fruits, of which love is central. Faith is considered separately below. Here the point is only the difference between the centrality of love for Wesley and of faith for Luther. Both saw faith and love as intimately related, but for Luther faith was the fundamental determinant of Christian life; for Wesley, it was love.

One reason for Wesley's emphasis on love is that he saw its connection with moral earnestness as tighter than that of faith. One can certainly argue that the recipients of faith, out of gratitude for the gift, will strive to do what good they can. But the expression of faith *can* be relief in being freed from the burden of the law and a more relaxed attitude toward works. Love of God and neighbor, on the other hand, immediately involves serving them however one can. It was of utmost importance to Wesley that Christian faith does not set the moral law aside.

In the sermon under consideration, Wesley made it clear that all that was characteristic of the "almost Christian" will characterize the "altogether Christian" as well. The disciplined effort to use every minute in the best possible way is not reduced by love. The life described as almost Christian is the outward form of Christianity which is now imbued with the true Christian spirit. The outward form does not become unimportant.

Indeed, love generates a righteousness that exceeds that of the scribes and Pharisees even in extent![13] Most important, it exceeds especially in fulfilling the spirit as well as the letter of the law.[14] But the interest in obeying even commandments that the Scribes and Pharisees neglected shows something of Wesley's distinctive spirit.

A Critique of Wesley's Doctrine of Love

Most Wesleyans celebrate the centrality of love in Wesley's theology and continue that tradition. But Wesley's own formulations are problematic in five respects, especially in their excessive rigor.

(1) There is no doubt that according to the Bible we should love God with our whole being. But there is some doubt as to whether any Biblical writer ever meant the peculiar state of being Wesley describes. Does this love take up *all* the affections and fill the *entire* capacity of the soul? If so, how could there also be love of neighbor? Or if we explain the way in which it takes up all the affections and fills the entire capacity of the soul as compatible with many other things going on in the soul at the same time, how can it employ the

utmost extent of all one's faculties? The whole account suggests that thinking about God dominates conscious experience continuously. This is absurd and incompatible with much else that Wesley writes, but one cannot easily say that it is not intended. With another writer, one might dismiss it as unimportant rhetorical excess, but not with Wesley.

Wesley is surely wrong in believing that a Christian love of God excludes the enjoyment of food and friends or longing for mutual love with other human beings. One could argue that if Wesley had allowed his enjoyment and longing to block his service of God and human beings, then his Christian love of God and neighbor would not be whole. But Wesley, with all his severity of self-criticism, does not accuse himself of that.

Wesley's error was a serious one. It had damaging consequences for his own life. It has evoked both despair and self-deception in others. It has led many to dismiss him and miss the large truth of what he offered. But it can be corrected without challenging the centrality of love. Indeed, a more reasonable understanding of human love of God can allow it to become central to all Christian thinking in a healing and enlivening way.

(2) It is only on the basis of this rigoristic understanding of the love of God that Wesley could draw a sharp line between the "altogether Christian" and the "almost Christian." The "almost Christian" has "a sincere view of pleasing God in all things: in all his conversation, in all his actions; in all he does or leaves undone. This design . . . runs through the whole tenor of his life. This is the moving principle, both in his doing good, his abstaining from evil, and his using the ordinances of God."[15] Could not this be understood, in fully Biblical terms, to be an expression of the love of God?

The Aldersgate experience led Wesley to see that something more was possible. This brought a fullness of feeling to the already existing motivation to please God. He not only *knew* that God loves, he also *felt* that love. This distinction is important. But should it be erected into the boundary between loving God in a Christian way and not?

Wesley himself paid a high price for having taken this step. Repeatedly he examined his own experience in light of his beliefs, and he found it wanting. In 1739, several months after the Aldersgate experience and two years before preaching "The Almost Christian," he wrote in his diary as follows:

My friends affirm that I am mad, because I said I was not a Christian a year ago. I affirm I am not a Christian now. Indeed, what I might have been I know not, had I been faithful to the grace, then given, when, expecting nothing less, I received such a sense of the forgiveness of my sins as till then I never knew. But that I am not a Christian at this day I as assuredly know as that Jesus is the Christ.

For a Christian is one who has the fruits of the Spirit of Christ, which (to mention no more) are love, peace, joy. But these I have not. I have not any love of God. I do not love either the Father or the Son. Do you ask how do I know whether I love God? I answer by another question, "How do you know whether you love me?" Why, as you know whether you are hot or cold. You *feel* this moment that you do or do not love me. And I *feel* this moment I do not love God; which therefore I *know* because I *feel* it. There is no word more proper, more clear, or more strong.

And I know it also by St. John's plain rule, "If any man love the world, the love of the Father is not in him." For I love the world. I desire the things of the world, some or other of them, and have done all my life. I have always placed some part of my happiness in some other of the things that are seen. Particularly in meat and drink, and in the company of those I loved. For many years I have been, yea, and still am, hankering after a happiness in loving and being loved by one or another. And in these I have from time to time taken more pleasure than in God.[16]

This was not a passing whimsy. In fact he continued to judge himself, at least at times, by the standard of a kind of love he ordinarily lacked—a kind, incidentally, that must be rare indeed. Twenty-seven years later, in a moment of depression, he wrote this in a letter to his brother, Charles, on June 27, 1766 :

I do not feel the wrath of God abiding on me; nor can I believe it does. And yet (this is the mystery) I do not love God. I never did. Therefore I never believed in the Christian sense of the word. Therefore I am only an honest heathen, a proselyte of the Temple, one of the God-fearers. And yet to be so employed of God! and so hedged in that I can neither get forward nor backward! Surely there never was such an instance before, from the beginning of the world![17]

Wesley himself was eventually led by his own experience and by what he saw in others to change his mind. He realized that he had judged too severely the zealous striver to be Christian whom he had called the "almost Christian." Instead of identifying this stage as pre-Christian, he came to call it "the faith of a servant." In 1788 he wrote:

> Whoever has attained this, the faith of a servant, . . . 'feareth God and worketh righteousness,' in consequence of which he is in a degree (as the Apostle observes), 'accepted with him.' . . . Even one who has gone thus far in religion, who obeys God out of fear, is not in any wise to be despised, seeing 'the fear of the Lord is the beginning of wisdom.' Nevertheless he should be exhorted not to stop there; not to rest till he attains the adoption of sons; till he obeys out of love, which is the privilege of all the *children* of God.[18]

Wesley realized that this was an important change in his theology. Already in 1774 it led him to revise the original journal entries in which he had asserted that he was not a Christian before Aldersgate. It is clear, therefore, that the mature Wesley did not view the heartwarming experience there as a conversion in the sense in which it has often been interpreted.[19]

It may be that many of Wesley's converts had deeper feelings of love than did Wesley himself. He seems, indeed, to have been temperamentally distanced from strong feeling. But to our eyes this is a psychological matter, and no particular temperament is required in order to be a Christian. We can appreciate Wesley's hunger for deeper religious feelings. But we must agree with Wesley's long-delayed acceptance of the judgment of those friends who believed that what Wesley called the "almost Christian," himself before Aldersgate, was already a Christian. A sincere desire to please God in all things is a way of loving God with all one's heart, soul, mind, and strength, whatever the feeling tone that accompanies it.

(3) Wesley identified one valid form of Christian life with the requirement on all Christians. This form was that of rigorous discipline. We saw above that he seized onto Matthew's account of Jesus as saying that our righteousness should exceed that of the scribes and Pharisees. In fact, however, Wesley did not advocate studying the Jewish law of the time of Jesus and observing all its moral teachings in detail. His real intention was that we should now scrupulously do all the good we can while avoiding all evil. That meant that we should not play or rest unnecessarily. We should always seek out some way to serve instead. We should organize our time as efficiently as possible to this end.

This is not bad advice for many. Some people do organize their time effectively so as to accomplish a great deal of good. Others, though generally well-meaning, never get their act together. On the whole, the former life-style is surely better than the latter. On the other hand, there are many other types of Christians. There are fun-loving people whose *joie de vivre* gives enjoyment to those around them. There are people of a contemplative temperament who may do relatively little overtly in the world but who emanate a spiritual depth that is contagious. There are people who are spontaneously loving in an emotional way to whom we turn when we need comfort. These people do not love God less than the disciplined activists. The church needs people of many temperaments and life-styles.

This does not remove the test of loving one's neighbor. That can be applied to disciplined activists, to fun-lovers, to contemplatives, and to the emotionally gifted. Do they really care what happens to others? Do the others about whom they care include strangers and "enemies" as well as congenial friends? This is a real and valid test to be applied especially to ourselves. It does not mean that only one lifestyle is acceptable or that any one style is right for all. Furthermore, it does not excuse anyone from obeying basic principles of morality as these grow out of the concern for the neighbor. Wesley is quite correct that a concern that is not expressed in righteous action is not the love of which the Bible speaks.

(4) Wesley distinguished too sharply between our love for God and our love for neighbor. Of course he saw both as stemming from God's love for us and the work of the Holy Spirit within us, and he rightly emphasized the importance of both. Against John Norris, who taught that God should be the only object of our love, he wrote this in his sermon on "The Love of God": "Not that God is so to be the only object of our love as to exclude his creatures from a subordinate share of it. . . . Nay, the love God constraineth those in whose hearts it is shed abroad to love what bears his image. And we cannot suppose any love forbidden by God which necessarily flows from this love of him."[20] Indeed, "if we love him we cannot but love one another, as Christ loved us."[21] Furthermore, he showed that the love of the creature may tend to the love of God, and said that whatever "tends to the love of God is no more forbidden than that which flows from it."[22]

Clearly, for Wesley, love of God and neighbor require one another and support one another. Nevertheless, the two loves remain quite distinct. The love of God expresses itself in works of piety, focusing on prayer and worship. The love of neighbor is expressed in works of mercy. The works of piety do not include the works of mercy. These are a separate set of relationships, supplementing what is directly entailed in loving God. The relation of the two loves presented in Wesley is less intimate than that in the New Testament. In Matthew's account of the final judgment, the judge asks not how absorbed one has been in thinking about God, in prayer, and in worship, but how one has served one's needy neighbors. Indeed, in the New Testament as a whole, there is very little about a love for God that is distinguishable in its expression from neighbor love.

Wesley's own understanding of God and the world should have taken him in the same direction. All things live and move and have their being in God. To love the God in whom are all things is surely far more than loving some particular things at the expense of others. It calls for disinterested care for *all* the creatures that contribute to the divine life. But it is precisely through benefiting these creatures that we honor and benefit God.

In order to say this unequivocally, however, one must affirm that God is affected by what happens to the creatures, especially the human ones. Much that Wesley said cuts in this direction. He stated that the scriptural assertion that God experiences joy at a person's conversion was an appropriate "representation."[23] In the formulation of Randy L. Maddox, Wesley insisted "that a God who did not take into account the changing response of humanity would cease to be unchangeably just and gracious."[24] This would imply that what happens in the world affects God, and that what is unchanging is God's character of justice and grace that opens God to all that happens.

On the other hand, Wesley was not willing to depart from the tradition on this point. This tradition had denied that God can be affected by what happens in the world. God was held to be without "passions." The denial of passions to God was present in the Anglican Articles of Religion, and Wesley did not delete this. This deletion was left to the American Methodists, who wisely made it.

Once it is affirmed that God suffers with us in our suffering and rejoices with us in our joys, then works of mercy can be understood to be also works of piety. Through giving joy to the neighbor they contribute to God's joy. Wesley's thought leads in this direction. His reluctance to change traditional affirmations about God held him back.

This reluctance went so far as to affect his understanding of Jesus. Because Jesus was God, in Wesley's view, Jesus had no passions! To have passions meant for him to be receptive of the feelings of others, therefore, not in complete control of what one felt. In his commentary on John 11:33, which asserts that Jesus troubled himself over Lazarus' death, he stated that Jesus' affections "were not properly passions, but voluntary emotions, which were wholly in his own power."[25] Clearly, if he would not recognize that Jesus was affected by the condition of people around him, he could not assert that what we do to our neighbor we do also to God. In this unwillingness to let go of traditional philosophical theology even when it required some distortion of the biblical story, we cannot and should not follow him. We should develop instead the implications of his more original thought.

(5) Wesley did not discuss the importance of loving ourselves. His rigorist self-criticism for caring for personal enjoyments suggests a rejection of self as an object of love. If he had affirmed love of self, he might well have appreciated his love of food and companionship instead of condemning himself for normal and healthy enjoyment.

Wesley was not extreme in his rejection of love of self. He did not criticize the eagerness for personal salvation which includes happiness as well as holiness. On this point there was no self-criticism. He did not call for willingness to be damned for the glory of God. He did not ask penitents to inflict suffering on themselves. His asceticism was only for the sake of more effectively serving others. Furthermore, Wesley was aware of the dangers of scrupulosity. He knew from personal experience the risk of enhancing doubt and anxiety in oneself by too severe self-judgment. He sought comfort and assurance, joy and peace for himself. As a skilled pastor he tried to dispense these to others.

Nevertheless, we can hardly avoid faulting Wesley for being too hard on himself. Instead of thanking God for the wholesome pleasures of ordinary life, he accused himself of relishing them too much. Instead of seeing his own enjoyments as contributing joy to God, he treated them as a distraction from loving God. His own understanding of God's presence in himself and his inclusion in God should have prevented him from falling into this dualism, but it did not.

One may well argue that Wesleyans in our day have moved too far toward self-love. Complacent self-indulgence may be a far greater problem with us than failure to love ourselves. Hence Wesley's emphasis on loving God and neighbor rather than ourselves is a needed corrective. However, just this dualism will block the hearing of Wesley's call for love. We may have exaggerated the priority of self-love by saying that only those who love themselves can love others. It may be equally true that only those who love others can love themselves. But we are not wrong in insisting that as God loves all, so we also should love all, including ourselves, and that the enjoyment of all is enjoyed by God.

Faith as "The Evidence of Things Unseen"

Although faith is not at the center of Wesley's theology, it stands next to that center. There is no love without faith. Hence, how faith is to be understood is of utmost importance.

Wesley's distinctive understanding of faith emerged gradually as his personal reflection and experience developed. In his youth and through his days at Oxford and in Georgia, he understood faith as assent to the truth of Christian teaching. It was Peter Böhler who taught him to understand it instead as trusting confidence in God. This enabled him to appreciate and appropriate much of the teaching and spirit of the Reformers. However, this shift in focus never led Wesley to doubt the importance of right beliefs as an essential element of faith. In the 1740s Wesley's own orginal contribution to the understanding of faith emerged, relating his thought to the dominant intellectual currents of his day.[26]

In Wesley's time empiricism had triumphed in philosophy. This meant that there was a sharp limitation to what is experienced. All primary experience is sensory and gives us only objects of sense. The mind could abstract ideas from the deliverances of sense and could reason about them. Hence much could be believed that was not seen or heard. But it was necessary to make a sharp distinction between what is directly experienced and what is believed on the basis of argument.

This empiricism seems to make belief in God a matter of inference. We believe in God because we observe things in the world that require supernatural explanation, or we see a need to name an external cause of the world as a whole. No one has claimed that God is experienced through the physical senses; so if this sense experience is our only direct access to what is not ourselves, God must be an inference from it.

This leads to a complex process. Once the inference to God is established, the reliability of the Bible as source of information about God and what God has done can be considered. Again, the reasoning will be inferential. There can be no appeal to the work of the Holy Spirit in confirming the truth of the Scripture until the reality of the Holy Spirit is established by inferential reasoning. One main reason for the decline in the convincing power of Christian faith has been that the elaborate arguments constructed to defend it in an empiricist context appear *ad hoc*. It seems that beliefs that arose in a quite different cultural context are not able to justify themselves effectively when that context changes.

Wesley was deeply dissatisfied with this sort of rational defense of Christian belief. It did not touch the heart. He was convinced, in any case, that the Bible speaks of a much more immediate, experiential relation between the believer and God. Only a more immediate knowledge of God and Christian truth could effect the deep changes in actual life for which Wesley longed.

Wesley was convinced that perception need not be limited to the bodily senses. The spirit could also perceive. Whereas bodily perception was oriented to the physical world, the perceptive capacities of the spirit are oriented to the spiritual world. Unfortunately, in the fallen condition of human beings, this perception is virtually absent. Its restoration by the Holy Spirit is of great importance to Wesley's account of salvation. In "The Great Privilege of Those that are Born of God" he wrote that before one is born of God,

> although he subsists by him in whom all that have life 'live and move and have their being', yet he is not *sensible* of God. He does not *feel*, he has no inward consciousness of his presence. He does not perceive that divine breath of life without which he cannot subsist a moment. . . .
>
> Hence he has scarce any knowledge of the invisible world, as he has scarce any intercourse with it. Not that it is far off. No; he is in the midst of it: it encompasses him round about. . . . Only the natural man discerneth it not; partly because he has no spiritual senses, whereby alone we can discern the things of God; partly because so thick a veil is interposed as he knows not how to penetrate.
>
> But when he is born of God, born of the Spirit, how is the

manner of his existence changed! His whole soul is now sensible of God, . . . all the senses of the soul being now awake, and capable of 'discerning' spiritual 'good and evil'.[27]

Wesley's fullest account of this important element in his episte-mology is in *An Earnest Appeal to Men of Reason and Religion*:

> Seeing our ideas are not innate, but must all originally come from our senses, it is certainly necessary that you have senses capable of discerning objects of this kind—not those only which are called 'natural senses', which in this respect profit nothing, as being altogether incapable of discerning objects of a spiritual kind, but *spiritual* senses, exercised to discern spiritual good and evil. It is necessary that you have the *hearing* ear, and the *seeing* eye, emphatically so called; that you have a new class of senses opened in your soul, not depending on organs of flesh and blood, to be 'the *evidence* of things not seen' as your bodily senses are of visible things, to be the avenues of the invisible world, to discern spiritual objects, and to furnish you with ideas of what the outward 'eye hath not seen, neither the ear heard.'[28]

The reference here to Hebrews 11:1 indicates the connection in Wesley's mind between these spiritual senses and faith. Elsewhere in the essay he wrote that faith is

> . . . the supernatural evidence of things invisible, not perceiv-able by eyes of flesh, or by any of our natural senses or faculties. Faith is that divine evidence whereby the spiritual man discerneth God, and the things of God. It is with regard to the spiritual world, what sense is with regard to the natural. It is the spiritual sensation of every soul that is born of God. . . .
>
> Faith . . . is the eye of the new-born soul. Hereby every true believer in God 'seeth him who is invisible'. . . .
>
> It is the ear of the soul, whereby a sinner 'hears the voice of the Son of God and lives'. . . .
>
> It is . . . the palate of the soul; for hereby a believer 'tastes the good word'. . . .
>
> It is the feeling of the soul, whereby a believer perceives . . . both the existence and the presence of Him in whom 'he lives, moves, and has his being'. . . .
>
> By this faith we are saved from all uneasiness of mind, from the anguish of a wounded spirit, from discontent, from fear and sorrow of heart. . . . This we know and feel, and therefore cannot but declare, saves every one that partakes of it, both from sin and misery, from every unhappy and every unholy temper.[29]

Much of what Wesley wrote about faith as he described the process of salvation does not explicitly refer to new spiritual sensations. Especially in the early years following Aldersgate, he often spoke of faith in ways similar to the Reformers, primarily as trust. However, there is no inconsistency. Wesley distinguished faith in general from specific forms of faith such as justifying faith. The latter are instances of spiritual "seeing" of particular truths combined with their existential appropriation:

> Faith in general is a divine, supernatural . . . 'evidence' or conviction 'of things not seen', not discoverable by our bodily senses as being either past, future, or spiritual. Justifying faith implies, not only a divine evidence or conviction that 'God was in Christ, reconciling the world unto himself', but a sure trust and confidence that Christ died for *my* sins, that he loved *me*, and gave himself for *me*.[30]

In the minutes of the First Annual Conference, 1744, a similar reference is made to repentance as well: "Faith . . . is a spiritual sight of God and the things of God. Therefore, repentance is a low species of faith, *i.e.* a supernatural sense of an offended God."[31]

The relation of faith and love is made clearer against this background. Without faith, God is only an inference. The kind of love we can have for that whose reality we only infer is certainly limited. God works in us whether we perceive this working or not, but God's grace can inspire love only as we become aware of it. As our spiritual eyes are opened to God's gracious working in all things, our whole way of understanding ourselves in relation to God is changed. This too can awaken a love that has an emotional dimension.

For Wesley it is not the new perceptions as such that are of primary importance. They are essential to the emergence of the kind of love that is authentically Christian. And it is that love that expresses itself necessarily in service of God and humanity.

A Critique of Wesley's Doctrine of Faith

Wesley's understanding of faith as a new way of seeing reality is of great worth. We should recover it in our changed situation. We too often think of Christian beliefs as something that can be added peripherally to our secular ones by an act of will. Or we think of them as another way to formulate what we believe on other grounds. To see the world through Christian glasses is to see it differently, to see features that are otherwise hidden. Any true conversion brings about new perceptions as well as new attitudes, emotions, and ways of acting.

Wesley's way of explaining these new perceptions is fascinating. It combines elements of two traditions in an original way.[32] There is first the Aristotelian tradition Wesley learned at Oxford, with its insistence, in Wesley's words, that "our senses are the only source of those ideas, upon which all our knowledge is founded. Without ideas of some sort or other we could have no knowledge, and without our senses we could have no ideas."[33] This empiricism was confirmed for Wesley by his reading of Locke and theologians who adopted and adapted Locke's thought. There is, second, the intuitionist tradition, known to Wesley especially through the Cambridge Platonists. This tradition insisted that there is immediate knowledge of the spiritual world, that this is not all secondary or inferential.

Although these traditions were generally viewed as mutually exclusive alternatives, Wesley combined them. He agreed with the intuitionists that there is direct knowledge of spiritual matters, although he limited this to believers. On the other hand, he avoided the technical use of "intuition." Instead, he affirmed that there are *spiritual* senses, alongside the physical ones, that give the same access to spiritual matters that the physical senses provide of the physical one. Wesley thought these additional organs of direct perception were brought into effective being by the Holy Spirit in conjunction with justification and the new birth.

Despite the theoretical interest we may take in this analysis, few today will find it convincing. It affirms a radical difference between the bases of natural and of spiritual knowledge that does not fit our experience. We can hardly avoid being skeptical of the existence of this second set of senses. And Wesley himself had difficulty with his own theory. In the same letter to his brother, quoted above, Wesley went on to say: "If I ever have had that *faith*, it would not be so strange. But I never had any other evidence of the eternal or invisible world than I have now; and that is none at all, unless such as faintly shines from reason's glimmering ray. I have no direct witness."[34]

What is seen and heard by the Christian seems to involve the same eyes and ears as those employed by others. The difference lies in what these eyes see, and what these ears hear, and how what is seen and heard is interpreted. Since Kant we have become aware that the mind is active in the selection and organization even of the data of the senses. People with different histories do not see and hear the same things even when they are in the same location. To explain difference, therefore, we do not have to introduce an additional set of organs.

John Hick, in *Faith and Knowledge*,[35] employed the insights of analytic philosophy to describe three levels of perceiving that characterize contemporary people. First, one may see the world only as natural. Second, one may see it also as moral. Third, one may see it religiously, inclusive, of course, of the natural and moral dimensions.

To take a simple example, consider a situation in which someone is threatening to jump from a high building. Typically a crowd gathers to watch. Some of them are there simply for the excitement. One does not see a man jump to his death every day! If he delays very long, the crowd may grow weary of waiting and begin to yell, "Jump!"

Others who are present may view the situation ethically. They experience it as morally wrong for the crowd to yell and even for people to gather out of idle interest. Unless one can help, one should move on. The moralists may believe that suicide is always wrong, or they may hold that the man should be free to make his own decision. In the former case they may offer their services to the police, if they think they can help. Whichever judgment they hold about suicide, they may try to silence the crowd or even to disperse it. The point here is that they experience the situation differently from those who see it as an occasion for a novel and interesting experience. They cannot provide evidence that their perceptions are better, but they certainly experience them to be so.

The religious perspective is more like the ethical than the natural one. Indeed, it includes the ethical within it. But although it condemns the crowd morally, it feels for its individual members and for the poverty of their lives that leads them to act in this despicable way. The religious person seeks to understand these people and to love them despite their sinful actions. She forgives even as she judges. They are children of God. She prays for God to be with them and enlighten them even while she may join the moralists in trying to silence or disperse them. The man who is threatening to jump is also a child of God. Whatever her moral judgment, she prays for God to be with him, to deter him from any foolish or immoral action. She asks that God's will be done even in this situation. The suffering of the lonely and miserable man draws forth her compassion and she tries to surround him with her love asking that he may also know God's love.

To become a Christian can be understood as beginning to experience the world in a religious way of this sort. It leads to selecting different features of what is experienced through the senses for attention. It interprets the selected features in distinctive ways. It clothes what it sees with different meanings and emotions. And accordingly the actions that follow are different.

This way of understanding the distinctiveness of Christian perceptions can function without challenging the empiricist principle that the mind has no data to work with except those that come through the sense organs. It shows that this does not limit perceptions to the merely natural sphere. But the principle that all perception is foundationally sensuous is not beyond challenge. Such a challenge can provide a position that is still closer to Wesley's. To explain this I appeal to my own philosophical tradition of process thought.

Process philosophy argues that sense perception is only a specialized form of a more general phenomenon. Even sense perception depends on prior, nonsensuous perception. To understand what this is, consider the relation of a moment of human experience not to the data of the senses but to the sense organs themselves. One does not, ordinarily, see the eye or hear the ear, or have any other sensory relation to them. Yet surely there is a relation. If the events in the eye had no causal efficacy in the experience, there would be no seeing of external objects.

Many people agree to this, but think of the relation to the sense organs as a purely material causation, fundamentally different from perception. Certainly it is not conscious, but from the process perspective the line between conscious and nonconscious perception is not so sharp or radical. One way to understand the difference, a way that does not separate causation from perception altogether, is to think that while influences are coming into experience from everywhere, they become conscious only when they are highly concentrated and organized as in the case of the sense organs or when one feels pain in some part of the body. For example light impacts the body all over, and this has some effect on our experience. But only the eye is so organized as to be specially receptive of the light. Consciousness of light depends on the eye.

The clearest instance of conscious nonsensory perception is our awareness in one moment of antecedent moments of our own experience. Sometimes we call this memory and treat it as a phenomenon quite distinct from both perception and causation. But process thinkers see all of these as diverse examples of one fundamental reality, the way events influence other events. In this interpretation, to perceive something is to be influenced by it. Generally the influence in my present experience of recently past ones is not conscious, but it is not impossible to attend to it. I can then see how extensively the present experience reenacts the earlier one, and yet, how other influences within it, and its own response, bring about differences.

If what flows into the present experience is fundamentally nonsensory, and if only some of these influences come from sense organs and bring about sensory experience, then we can understand that much of our experience of the world outside our body is also nonsensory. Sometimes we call this extrasensory. We can also understand that if God is present and working in us, as Wesley (and also process philosophy) affirms, there is nonsensory perception of God all the time. The question is whether one can discriminate God's work from other forces operative in experience and become aware of it. If so, then something much like what Wesley describes is possible. Instead of speaking of new spiritual senses, we can think of nonsensuous experience of the divine presence in our lives and awareness of its salvific effects.

Wesley relied on traditional Aristotelian philosophy and the eighteenth-century British empiricism represented by John Locke. We can today make use of analytic philosophy, or process philosophy, or both, or neither. What the engagement with Wesley's doctrine of faith calls for is our creative reflection about how, in becoming Christian, we come to perceive reality in a new way. If we clarify the distinctiveness of the Christian vision of reality, and if it increases and deepens love of God and neighbor, then we can strengthen one another in that vision and offer it enthusiastically to others. This would be a Wesleyan theology for our time.

We can also understand why the emergence of the new vision or way of perceiving is the work of grace, or of the Holy Spirit. One cannot argue either oneself or another person into a different way of seeing the world. We see what we see, and we usually do not recognize that there is another way of seeing until that new way of seeing begins to dawn on us. If we come to notice the work of grace in ourselves and others, that will itself be the work of grace in us. On the other hand, Wesley is equally sure, and we can agree, grace is not irresistible. It accomplishes its purposes as we allow it to do so and cooperate with it. That allowing and that cooperating are also the working of grace within us. But God does not save us without our participation.

CHAPTER 4

The Way of Salvation, I:
God's Pardon

Wesley as a Reformation Thinker

Chapter 1 located Wesley as a Reformation thinker. It showed that for the Reformation the central focus was "the way of salvation." When this is our concern today, we rightly return to Luther, Calvin, Wesley, and other figures of the Reformation period, alongside the Roman Catholic thinkers who debated with them. Although there have continued to be vigorous debates on these matters during the nineteenth and twentieth centuries, they have been largely derivative from the positions of these Reformers and the formulations of Roman Catholic thought, in reaction to the early Reformers, at the Council of Trent. In the nineteenth and twentieth centuries the most original Christian thinkers have been more concerned to justify Christianity as a whole in the context of radically changed worldviews.

Unfortunately, the shift of attention away from the way of salvation in the work of the major thinkers of the nineteenth century was accompanied by a fading of interest among Christians generally. The language in which the discussion was carried on then is rarely used now. The subtlety and rigor of thought of the Reformation in regard to Christian salvation has been largely lost, certainly among United Methodists. Psychological categories that have superseded theological ones in popular Protestantism are far less exact and carefully related to one another.

Wesley himself bears some of the responsibility for the shift from theology to psychology in the American churches in general and in United Methodism in particular. He placed a far greater weight on the actual experience of the Christian than had Luther or Calvin. Of course, experience enters into all theology. If Luther's discovery in the Bible of the doctrine of justification by faith had not been accompanied by an intense experience of relief and release, his theological and institutional work would not have been organized around this idea. Nevertheless, for Luther it was the objective truth that he found in the Bible, rather than the subjective experience, that provided the center of his theology. He did not appeal to his experience as evidence for the doctrine, nor did he study what happened in the experience of others.

For Wesley, too, the Biblical teaching was decisive. But he was convinced that unless it became effective in human life it remained abstract and useless. He constantly examined his own experience and that of others to see whether and how the Biblical teaching was realized. His way of expounding the teaching was guided by what he found. The empirical study of conversion experiences that constituted a major source of nineteenth-century American psychology of religion was a continuation of one aspect of Wesley's work. It broke with Wesley, of course, in abandoning the language of the Bible in the description of these experiences and substituting psychological categories. This led in turn to abandoning the belief structure and anthropology of the Bible in favor of new views of human experience generated by a variety of schools of psychology.

Psychological categories are too convincing and too deeply entrenched in our culture for a simple return to Biblical or theological ones to be possible. The effort to make that move leads to separating the way people are taught to think about their faith from the way they interpret life in general. That ghettoization of Christianity is more profoundly unWesleyan than is its psychologization. Nevertheless, the latter, too, spells doom for a vital Christianity. Christians lose the capacity to critique psychological categories from a Christian perspective. Instead, Christianity is absorbed into a way of thinking and relating to people and the world that is determined by a different set of assumptions and commitments. Only those aspects of Christianity survive that can justify themselves by these different standards. Because these standards are psychological, the already dangerous tendency toward individualism in Protestantism, and especially in the Wesleyan tradition, is accentuated, and the individual is now viewed in a fundamentally autonomous way. "God" becomes a problematic term. Faith as a trusting attitude may remain, but what Wesley meant by faith disappears.

There cannot be real renewal within the Wesleyan movement without rigorous reflection on the Christian life. It is doubtful that such reflection will be fruitful for Wesleyans if it does not include serious study of Wesley's own views. But it is also doubtful that those views can be appropriated today without extensive translation and revision. What form of translation and what form of revision would serve the revitalization of the United Methodist Church is the concern of this chapter and the next.

Wesley's understanding of the way of salvation must be seen as a single coherent theory. Nevertheless, for practical purposes I have divided the material, taking Wesley's own cue from his sermon on "The New Birth":

> If any doctrines within the whole compass of Christianity may be termed fundamental they are doubtless these two—the doctrine of justification and that of the new birth: the former relating to that great work which God does *for us*, in forgiving our sins; the latter to the great work which God does *in* us, in renewing our fallen nature. In order of time neither of these is before the other. In the moment we are justified by the grace of God through redemption that is in Jesus we are also 'born of the Spirit'; but in order of thinking, as it is termed, justification precedes the new birth. We first conceive his wrath to be turned away, and then his Spirit to work in our hearts.[1]

Since assurance is the subjective accompaniment of justification, this chapter on God's pardon treats assurance as well as justification. Since the new birth initiates the process of sanctification, Chapter 5 treats sanctification as well as the new birth.

Human Sinfulness

For Wesley the whole account of the way of salvation made no sense without the assumption that human beings are in fundamental need of salvation. This is traditionally the doctrine of original sin and human depravity. Wesley did not insist upon this language, but he did insist upon the radical sinfulness of human nature.

The natural condition of humanity as fallen can only be perceived from the perspective of Christian faith. Of course, the fact that human beings do terrible things is visible to all. But the appraisal of the human condition in general depends upon the norm by which it is judged. If the norm arises from ideas about what constitutes socially constructive behavior, for example, then the fact that such behavior exists, that it is, indeed, widespread, means that human beings are naturally capable of virtue as well as vice. The issue is simply that of the relative strength of these two tendencies. This is the position characteristic of the natural perspective.[2]

But in Wesley's view the Christian could not judge human nature in this way. The Christian knows that righteousness consists in the love of God and neighbor. When even the most virtuous pagans along with most baptized Christians are judged by that standard, it turns out that they are very far from righteous.

This is not simply a matter of people's lack of exertion of natural capacities. The deeper truth is that by nature people cannot know God in such a way as to love God. They may infer from their physical senses that the universe has an order that points to a powerful ruler. But this knowledge does not evoke love. Within the limits of the natural condition, there is simply no basis for loving God. There is, indeed, no basis in this context for supposing that one should love God.

From the Christian point of view, much that is perfectly acceptable from the natural perspective is sinful. For example, much that might be called healthy pride and self-assertion by the pagan is in Christian perspective the idolatry of self. Where God is not loved, the world is. This leads to the gratification of natural desires of the body and of the imagination and to the quest for praise.

Wesley's sermon on "Original Sin,"[3] from which the above points are drawn, was not based on the story of the fall of Adam. Of course, Wesley accepted that account uncritically, as he did Biblical stories in general. But his argument did not depend on that. His sermon is based on the story of Noah, and the text is Genesis 6:5: "The LORD saw that the wickedness of humankind was great in the earth, and that every inclination of the thoughts of their hearts was only evil continually." Wesley's basic argument was that our natural condition today is unchanged from that described in the text.

If this were his entire position, then becoming a Christian would be a radical event indeed! It would involve an instantaneous reversal from a totally depraved condition to one of love of God and humanity. Wesley did want to emphasize the change. But he did not see it in this way. Even in this sermon, in which his overwhelming emphasis was on the impotence of the natural human being to take any steps toward Christian righteousness, he introduced repeated qualifications.

He began one passage by re-emphasizing the totality of the corruption of human nature: "But was there not good mingled with the evil? Was there not light intermixed with the darkness? No, none at all: 'God saw that the whole imagination of the heart' of man 'was *only* evil.'"[4] But then Wesley introduced this important qualification: "It cannot be denied but many of them, perhaps all, had good motions put into their hearts. For the spirit of God did then also 'strive with man,' if haply he might repent."[5]

It is clear, therefore, that although Wesley emphasized the corruption of human nature, he believed that in actual human beings there are impulses to good. Chapter 2 showed that these constitute prevenient (or preventing) grace or the living presence of the Holy Spirit. This working of grace does not by itself effect the faith apart from which no one knows and loves God. But it does lead toward that end in many ways. The "almost Christian" is a product of this working of prevenient grace. Thus among those who are not Christians one may distinguish not only important differences arising from "constitution and . . . education," but also differences "wrought by preventing grace."[6] The movement across the line to being an authentic Christian is supremely important, but it may be continuous with the working of grace that has brought one to that point.

Wesley's teaching here is not difficult to accept in our time. It *is* the case that what is regarded as sinful is a function of the norms by which we judge. The norm we confront in the New Testament, the norm of love, renders sinful much that does not otherwise appear so. The doctrine of the universal corruption of human nature results from this recognition.

The universal corruption of human nature is for Wesley an essential Christian doctrine apart from which the whole gospel becomes meaningless. If our nature were not corrupt, if we were truly free in our own strength to act righteously, we would have no need of a physician. But "the Christian Revelation speaks of nothing else but the great 'Physician' of our souls; nor can Christian Philosophy . . . be more properly defined than in Plato's word: . . . 'the only true method of healing a distempered soul.'"[7]

The fact of universal corruption points for Wesley, as its explanation, to the sin of Adam. Hence he affirms "original sin," using this term in titles, although rarely in the text of his writings.[8] Its secondary and derivative character in Wesley, however, indicates that contemporary Wesleyans, for whom the literal appeal to Adam is highly problematic, do not need to depart far from their mentor. The basic issue is whether humanity as a whole is wounded and diseased and needs a Physician.[9] If so, then the affirmation that the needed Physician is Jesus Christ can be made with conviction.

But what about guilt? Are people guilty for not doing what they do not even know they should do? This is a question that is inevitable for us. It was not strange to Wesley either. His answer was Yes and No.

Christians awakened to the true law of love realize that their lives have been sinful not only in particulars but as a whole. They share this sinfulness with the whole of humanity, but that does not render it less sinful. It is objectively wrong, a break with God. And it has objective consequences. For Wesley the primary consequence is mortality, both physical and spiritual. Since mortality is a suffering brought about by sin, Wesley calls it punishment, and he vigorously defends this language in his debate with John Taylor.[10]

Few today would agree that physical mortality in general, affecting both humans and animals, is a result of human sinfulness. But to see human spiritual death as the result of sinfulness, even when that sinfulness is simply part of the universal, given, situation, does make sense. Wesley also emphasized how the general condition of lack of love for God produces innumerable specific sins and evils that lead to widespread misery. That, too, makes sense for us as well.

But that still leaves open the question of guilt. The earlier Reformers had attributed collective guilt to all humankind. In Adam's sin the whole body of humanity sinned. Hence they emphasized universal human guilt accompanying universal depravity. The fate of an individual was not determined by personal sins, and all people deserved nothing but punishment. So in principle there was no reason to deny that infants too are guilty and deserving of eternal punishment.

Wesley drew back from this conclusion. He agreed that physical death is a punishment for the sin of Adam who was in some way the representative of all human beings. Hence death afflicts all people, including infants, independently of their personal sin. But spiritual or eternal death is inflicted only for actual sins. "I believe none ever did, or ever will, die eternally, merely for the sin of our first father."[11]

The particular form that Wesley's doctrine took appears to us somewhat ad hoc. It is a response to the formulations of his time. He insisted that no one would ever be condemned solely on account of original sin, even if all somehow participate in the guilt of that sin.[12] He went on to propose that whatever guilt of original sin may attach to us individually today, this was cancelled at birth as one benefit of

Christ's redemption.[13] To the extent that this represents his definitive judgment, the doctrine that all humanity is guilty because of Adam's sin ceases to function for Wesley except as a justification for suffering and death. The moral and soteriological consequences we suffer from the fall consist in the human propensity of nature to evil, not in any real or imputed guilt.

Wesley's struggle with these matters was in the context of a quite literal understanding of divine judgment after death. Most of us cannot think of God as imposing sufferings at that point that do not arise necessarily out of who and what we are. Hence, our reflections are likely to have a different tone. Nevertheless, we may be glad that Wesley rejected the punishment of infants, and we may also say both Yes and No to the general question of guilt attaching to unrecognized sinfulness.

The fullest and clearest case of guilt arises, as Wesley emphasized, when we individually, knowingly and willfully, do what we ought not to do. But are those the only instances in which we feel guilty? Certainly not. Many of these other cases may be ones that we regard as irrational and unhealthy. In these instances we need to be freed of guilt feelings rather than forgiven. But there is also a participation in collective guilt. In my case, I participate in the guilt of Southern whites for our collective crimes against blacks. I participate in the crimes of the United States in its support of repressive regimes in Latin America. I participate in the guilt of Christians for our vilification of the Jews. I participate in the guilt of the human species for what it has done to other species. When I suffer as a result of the evils in question, there is justice in that suffering.

Furthermore, I am not entirely innocent prior to the time that I am conscientized about these evils. Until I am conscientized I do not feel guilty for them. But when I become aware of the evil, I recognize that I have been objectively guilty even when I knew no better. I am likely to feel that I could and should have known better, but my objective guilt is not limited to my subjective refusal to see what I could have seen.

The same applies to learning the nature of true righteousness as love. As that conscientization takes place, I recognize that all my previous righteousness still participated in a fundamental self-centeredness and lovelessness. This had its consequences for me and for others. It was objectively sinful, and I now feel guilt for having participated in that sinful pattern of relationships. Its continuing negative consequences in my own life, and the life of those around me, appear to me as just.

Historically, the thrust of Wesley's theology was to move Christians toward emphasis on personal voluntary sins. It would be easy for us simply to follow that trajectory, abandoning the earlier ideas of collective guilt. My suggestion is that Wesley's own balance between collective and individual guilt is better, that it can be translated fruitfully into our situation, and that wrestling with it in this way is preferable to adopting the simplistic individualism into which much of the Wesleyan movement has fallen.

Justification

In one central respect Wesley's doctrine of justification stands outside the mainstream of his teaching about the way of salvation. Every other doctrine deals with the actual experience of people. In all of this experience God is present and active. His account is not psychological in the ordinary sense, but it describes what is going on in human beings in the process of becoming Christians. In contrast, the doctrine of justification does not speak of Christian experience. It speaks of what God does, not within human beings, but within the divine life itself.

For Wesley, however, nothing could be more important than what happens in the divine life. What happens in human beings depends entirely upon it. Since all human beings are hopelessly immersed in sin, their salvation depends on God, and first and foremost it depends on God's accepting them despite their sin. That acceptance is forgiveness, and that forgiveness or pardon is justification.

In the context in which Wesley thought, this objective occurrence in the life of God was of immense importance. Until it occurs, one is destined for Hell. Through it, Wesley explained in his sermon on "Justification by Faith," God acts "to remit the punishment due to our sins, to reinstate us in his favour, and to restore our dead souls to spiritual life, as the earnest of life eternal."[14]

Wesley followed the earlier Reformers closely in his doctrine of justification. The primary focus of his attention, like theirs, was on the conditions under which God pardons the sinner. In the language of the Reformation this discussion focuses on the relation to faith and works. Despite Wesley's strong emphasis on works in general, with respect to justification he followed the lead of the earlier Reformers in excluding them. God does not forgive us because of our works. God's pardon has nothing to do with what we deserve.

The occurrence of God's pardon has two conditions, one external and universal, and the other internal and personal. The former is the work of Christ. The latter is faith, defined by the Church of England as "a sure trust and confidence [. . .] that God both hath and will forgive our sins, that he hath accepted us again into his favor, [. . .] for the merits of Christ's death and Passion."[15] Wesley did not explain *how* the work of Christ leads to God's readiness to pardon, he only affirmed *that* this is the case. He did not explain *how* faith functions as a condition of God's pardon. He only affirmed *that* it does so. He did speculate in this latter regard that the specification of this condition works against human pride. He also emphasized that the condition God requires is one God makes it possible for human beings to fulfill. Strikingly, in his treatment of justification, Wesley did not discuss his own distinctive doctrine of faith as a spiritual seeing. Instead he quoted the official doctrine of the Church of England. It almost seems that on this doctrine he had nothing of his own to say.

I have summarized Wesley's sermon "Justification by Faith" baldly and objectively to clarify the sense in which his doctrine of justification repeats that of the earlier Reformers despite his differences at other points. One might draw the conclusion that Wesley was simply protecting himself from accusations of heresy by stating this Reformation doctrine in so conventional a way. But this would be a misunderstanding. The doctrine was of great importance to him.

For Wesley the inner growth of grace, bringing one to the Christian life and then to increasing holiness, depends on an objective ground. The lack of such a ground in mysticism was what led him to reject it. He needed to believe that something more was going on than he could discern within himself. The message that the work of Christ did for him what he could not do for himself was essential for his hope. He further needed to believe that the effects of Christ's work were not exhausted by the subjective experience of believers. It is the confidence that God has pardoned us that enables believers to grow in grace. *That* one is pardoned of all one's sins is the necessary objective ground of the effective working of grace in one's heart.

Despite this great similarity of Wesley's doctrine of justification to what he learned from the earlier Reformers, setting it in the context of his own thought gives it a different character. This becomes apparent when it is viewed within his overall account of the way of salvation. He summarized this in his sermon "On Working Out Our Own Salvation," whose title itself suggests a different approach to the topic:

> Salvation begins with what is usually termed (and very properly) 'preventing grace'; including the first wish to please God, the first dawn of light concerning his will, and the first slight transient conviction of having sinned against him. All these imply some tendency toward life, some degree of salvation, the beginning of a deliverance from a blind, unfeeling heart, quite insensible of God and the things of God. Salvation is carried on by 'convincing grace,' usually in Scripture termed 'repentance,' which brings a larger measure of self-knowledge, and a farther deliverance from the heart of stone. Afterwards we experience the proper Christian salvation, whereby 'through grace' we 'are saved by faith,' consisting of those two grand branches, justification and sanctification. By justification we are saved from the guilt of sin, and restored to the favour of God; by sanctification we are saved from the power and root of sin, and restored to the image of God.[16]

Read in light of Wesley's distinctive understanding of faith, it is clear that grace is working throughout to bring into being spiritual sight. The first wish to please God is connected with the first glimpses into God's loving reality. This brings about some awareness of God's will and therefore of one's failure to live by it. At this point the same activity of grace can be called "convincing" in that it convicts of sin. That is, the increased perception of who God is increases self-knowledge, and that is knowledge of how one has failed to be what one should.

One of the main functions of preaching was to provide the outward stimulus for the inward working of convincing grace. Again and again Wesley held up the actual lives of ordinarily good people for critical review against the full demands of the gospel of love. Repentance must precede justifying faith. For example, in his sermon on "The Way to the Kingdom,"[17] he took as his text Mark 1:15: "The kingdom of God is at hand: repent ye, and believe the gospel" (KJV).

He began by explaining that the Kingdom is true religion which, in turn, is a matter of the heart, a matter of loving God and neighbor. The nature of this love he portrays in glowing and demanding terms:

> Thou shalt delight thyself in the Lord thy God; thou shalt seek and find all happiness in him. He shall be 'thy shield, and thy exceeding

great reward', in time and in eternity. All thy bones shall say, 'Whom have I in heaven but thee? And there is none upon earth that I desire beside thee!'[18]

To love thy neighbor is

... to embrace with the most tender goodwill, the most earnest and cordial affection, the most inflamed desires of preventing or removing all evil and of procuring for him every possible good ... not only thy friend, thy kinsman, or thy acquaintance; not only the virtuous, the friendly, him that loves thee, that prevents or returns thy kindness; but every child of man, every human creature, every soul which God hath made.[19]

After describing Christian love in these extravagant terms, Wesley forced his hearers to consider how far their actual experience falls short of this. To know oneself as one is in relation to what one should be is repentance. This is a "lively conviction of thy inward and outward sins, of thy utter guiltiness and helplessness," and added thereto "sorrow of heart for having despised thy own mercies; remorse and self-condemnation."[20]

In later sermons, especially "The Spirit of Bondage and of Adoption," Wesley treated this situation as a distinct type of life, which he called the legal state. Those who know that God demands of them more than they are accomplishing struggle to obey. They continue to sin, but now unwillingly. In this sermon, on the other hand, this repentance is presented as the immediate condition for justifying faith. "One step more and thou shalt enter in. Thou dost 'repent'. Now, 'believe the gospel'."[21]

Finally, (through justifying grace) one sees spiritually that in spite of one's sin God loves her or him and, for the sake of Christ, forgives. The guilt one felt so keenly, as one saw what God's will truly is, dissolves. One knows oneself as accepted and loved by God. One is no longer helplessly bound to sin, but finds the beginnings of true love of God and other people emerging within one's heart.

Since, in Wesley's view, repentance precedes justifying faith, it seems to be another condition of justification alongside faith. This would seem to violate the Reformation slogan, "justification by faith alone." Yet Wesley did not believe that justifying faith could arise without repentance. One must recognize one's need for pardon before one can appropriate that pardon. This would seem to contradict the rejection of works as a condition for justification, because repentance, if it is authentic, necessarily produces fruits. Even if one cannot do what is truly good, the penitent person tries to change. If such efforts necessarily precede justification, the doctrine that faith alone is the condition is compromised.

Wesley struggled with this in two ways. First, he denied that the fruits of repentance had to precede justification. If the time between repentance and justification sufficed, he could not imagine that such fruits would not in fact occur. But the move from repentance to justification can be immediate. The fruits of repentance may not occur until after justification.

Second, he avoided verbally affirming repentance as an additional condition of justification by asserting that the relation was indirect. Repentance was a condition of faith, but only faith was the condition of justification. In his own mind, one suspects, this was not important. He did not conceive justifying faith as emerging out of the void. It was a new expression of the grace that had always been working. That there is an order to the movement of grace toward justifying faith does not take away from the fact that it is this, and this alone, that is the specific condition of justification.[22]

This paraphrase summary of Wesley's account of the way of salvation located justification in the context of the believer's experience. This is where it belongs for Wesley. Justification is not simply the objective fact that God pardons, nor is it simply a cognitive belief that this so. It involves an experience of being pardoned or knowing ourselves as pardoned—the sort of experience Wesley had at Aldersgate. It is not just the knowledge that Christ has taken away our guilt. It involves also becoming experientially free from that guilt.

This account has blurred one distinction. In the sermon on "Justification by Faith," Wesley presents faith as a condition, required by God for God's pardon. It seems that Christ's sacrifice does not suffice but must be supplemented by our meeting this additional condition. However, the definition of faith that he quotes from the Church of England can be read in another way. It seems rather to mean that God's forgiveness cannot be effective in our lives except as we have a sure confidence in its reality. This is a more appropriate way for a Wesleyan to understand the relation of faith and pardon, and the summary formulation above has adopted it. There is much in Wesley that supports this understanding. That is, rather than supposing that God withholds pardon until we meet a certain condition, whose relation to this pardon may be somewhat arbitrary, it is far more Wesleyan to think that our spiritual eyes are opened to the reality of God's pardon and that we seize this truth with confidence and joy.

The connection between God's pardon and Jesus' death was certainly important to Wesley, but many Wesleyans have found it puzzling. Does this connection mean that prior to the crucifixion God was unwilling or unable to pardon human beings? Why would a loving God require such suffering as a condition of pardoning creatures who are not personally responsible for their sin?

It is hard to determine Wesley's views on questions of this sort. His insistence *that* there is a relation between Jesus' sacrifice and God's pardon is clear, but his refusal to be drawn into theories about this connection leave alternatives open. In his view, the Jews lived under the covenant of grace before the time of Jesus and this covenant was given through Christ. Clearly Christ is salvifically at work superhistorically. Wesley sometimes refers to the lamb slain from the beginning of the world. He may mean that God has always been ready to forgive based on the eternal sacrifice or on foreknowledge of Jesus' death. Or he may mean that the historical event reveals something eternal about the Word. Through such strategies we could reconcile Wesley's insistence on the primacy of love in all God's dealings with the world with his affirmation that God's pardon is conditioned on Jesus' sacrifice.[23]

I would propose, however, a different move for Wesleyans. The proposals above are in danger of losing the concreteness of history. We can renew emphasis on that concreteness if we affirm that the life, death, and resurrection of Jesus introduced new possibilities in the relation between God and human beings and that our Christian lives and experience today depend on that historical event. This avoids suggesting that a previously angry God was mollified, but it retains the idea that the kind of reconciliation between God and human beings that became possible as a result of the Christ event, for those who live from it, is new.[24]

Assurance

The doctrine of assurance was characteristic of the Reformers as a whole. Against Catholic teaching that one could not be assured of one's salvation, the Protestants asserted that believers were assured of their justification. For Luther and Calvin, this was grounded in the objectivity of the saving act. The decision about one's salvation is God's, and it does not depend on any human act. Some might suppose that the consequence was that no one could know whether God had elected her or him. But Luther and Calvin thought of this in just the other way. One's very concern over whether one is of the elect is a sign that one is. One can cling to God's promises, sure that God does not fail.

Luther and Calvin believed that if salvation depends in any way on a human act, no one can ever be sure of having met the conditions. Just for this reason all would always lack assurance. Only if there are no conditions that must be met, can there be assurance. Faith, thus, is not really a condition of justification; it is rather the confidence that God will be gracious. That assurance is faith, and in faith is assurance.

For Wesley assurance of this kind was impossible and dangerous. Not only could people never be sure that their faith was sufficient, but also to separate faith from righteousness in this way cut the nerve of endeavor to become fully Christian. Furthermore, the idea that God would elect people without regard to their willingness, and especially that God would elect some for damnation, was abominable to him. He could not, therefore, take over this doctrine of assurance.

Because people's ultimate destiny is conditioned on their actual lives, no one can be assured about that. People cannot know what they will be or do tomorrow. Assurance for Wesley has to do with one's present condition.[25] Is one *now* justified and regenerate? That is, is one *now* a Christian? For Wesley it was very important that one not be uncertain about that. The whole movement of salvation depends on accurately and honestly knowing one's condition.

To know whether one is a Christian is essentially to know whether one has faith. Thus, assurance and faith are very closely connected in Wesley as in the earlier Reformers. But the earlier doctrine was very different from Wesley's. When one doubted one's faith, the earlier Reformers would point out that God is to be confidently trusted. One should attend to God's faithfulness rather than to one's subjective state. Assurance is not a feeling about one's own condition. It is a conviction about God.

In Wesley's time and context, the typical position was quite different. Salvation was not so often thought of as a status determined by God and independent of the quality of life. It was, indeed, very closely connected with that quality. Hence, whether one had authentic faith, and was therefore justified, was to be decided by whether the fruits of faith were manifest in one's life. These fruits are the evidence of one's faith. If they are clearly present, one may be assured that one is a Christian. Thus assurance was a rational deduction from the evidence.

Most of Wesley's critics affirmed only this indirect witness of the Spirit, that is, the evidence provided by the inner experience of love, joy, and peace and the outward expression of this in good works. Wesley never questioned the importance of this indirect witness to the working of the Spirit. Much of his preaching focused on the fruits of the Spirit. Where these were absent, he warned against trusting in any supposed direct witness. But he also warned against trusting the indirect witness in the absence of the direct witness.[26] One can deceive oneself about one's inner condition and can simulate good works without the real transformation effected by the Spirit.

Furthermore, the direct witness of the Spirit must precede the emergence of the fruits.[27] It is because one knows oneself to be forgiven that love, joy, and peace emerge in one's heart. To make the fruits the primary witness distorts this fundamental character of Christian experience. Hence, despite the massive objections raised against this doctrine, Wesley refused to back away from his emphasis on the importance of the direct witness of the Spirit.

Our question is how Wesley understood this direct witness. One clarifying passage can be found in his second sermon on "The Witness of the Spirit":

> I do not mean hereby that the Spirit of God testifies by any outward voice; no, nor always by an inward voice, although he may do this sometimes. Neither do I suppose that he always applies to the heart (though he often may) one or more texts of Scripture. But he so works upon the soul by his immediate influence, and by a strong though inexplicable operation, that the stormy wind and troubled waves subside, and there is a sweet calm; the heart resting as in the arms of Jesus, and the sinner being clearly satisfied that God is reconciled, that all his 'iniquities are forgiven, and his sins covered.'[28]

Wesley's reflection on these matters stemmed distinctively from his own Aldersgate experience. His account of that experience is worth examining again in this connection. "I felt I did trust in Christ, Christ alone for my salvation; and an assurance was given me that He had taken away *my* sins, even *mine*, and saved *me* from the law of sin and death."[29] Although Wesley's feeling of trust or faith directed to Christ can be distinguished from the gift of assurance with respect to his own condition, the two are presented as occurring together and seem almost inseparable. To trust Christ as savior is to trust that Christ is saving one. Perhaps "assurance" is stronger than "trust," but one can see why it was difficult for Wesley to think that one occurred without the other.

This way of understanding the relation of faith and assurance is supported in a letter to Richard Thompson:

> You add: 'Assurance is quite a distinct thing from faith. Neither does it depend upon the same agent. Faith is an act of my mind, assurance an act of the Holy Ghost.' I answer: (1) The assurance in question is no other than the full assurance of faith; therefore it cannot be a distinct thing from faith, but only so high a degree of faith as excludes all doubt and fear. (2) This *plerophory*, or full assurance, is doubtless wrought in us by the Holy Ghost, but so is every degree of true faith; yet the mind of man is the subject of both. I believe feebly; I believe without all doubt.[30]

Yet in the very next paragraph, Wesley seems to contradict this. "Your next remark is: 'The Spirit's witnessing that we are accepted cannot be the faith whereby we are accepted.' I allow it. A conviction that we are justified cannot be implied in justifying faith itself."[31]

If we are to make sense of both statements, we must recall that for Wesley justifying faith is only one form of faith. Therefore, the assurance occasioned by the Spirit's witness is a further stage of faith, one that the previous answer would suggest is a fuller and stronger faith. In the account of Aldersgate the justifying faith was the trust in Christ, the assurance was that his sins were taken away. In any case, for Wesley, justifying faith and the assurance that one is forgiven are experiential. They are themselves gifts of the Spirit. One experiences them as the working of that Spirit within oneself. Thus the experience of the Spirit is direct and immediate. It is not inferred from consequences related to it only indirectly.

It is only because there are faith and assurance as actual moments in experience that there are also the fruits. Thus faith and assurance are independent evidence of justification or of one's status as a child of God. Indeed, for the individual person they are the primary evidence, although for the observer the fruits are the more accessible and reliable form of evidence. And even the person in question will want this confirmation.

But one can be confident of one's faith and of what one believes in that faith only as one knows that it is of God. If we must suspend judgment until we observe later fruits, the faith will not produce those fruits. There must be an immediate self-evidence of the truth in the faith itself. In "The Witness of the Spirit, I," Wesley stated: "The Spirit of God does give a believer such a testimony of his adoption that while it is present to the soul he can no more doubt the reality of his sonship than he can doubt of the shining of the sun while he stands in the full blaze of his beams."[32]

This passage is highly suggestive of Wesley's view that faith is a matter of spiritual perceptions. This connection is made even more explicit later in the sermon:

> That soul is absolutely assured, 'This voice is the voice of God.' But yet he who hath that witness in himself cannot explain it to one who hath not. . . . Were there any natural medium to prove, or natural method to explain the things of God . . . , then the natural man might discern and know the things of the Spirit of God. But . . . 'they are spiritually discerned;' even by spiritual senses which the natural man hath not.[33]

Wesley's theory, then, is that the Holy Spirit brings into operation the spiritual senses and impresses certain truths on them. When this occurs the truths are as evident as is the sun to the one who looks at it. Thus the assurance is given with the truth. The Holy Spirit bears witness that we are children of God. One can, in this event, distinguish the moment of justifying faith from the assurance of one's condition, but the distinction is of minimal importance.

Nevertheless, Wesley did allow for a separation between justifying faith and assurance.[34] He was pressed to do so because some whom he recognized as authentic believers denied that they had the witness of the Spirit. He was forced to choose between rejecting their faith altogether and acknowledging that in exceptional circumstances there could be justifying faith without assurance. He chose the latter.

Furthermore, as he himself identified his Aldersgate experience more and more as one Christian experience within a longer Christian life, he saw that the particular form of assurance he had enjoyed there is not essential to justifying faith. Hence the distinction of faith and assurance became increasingly important. Wesley never gave up his desire that the faith of all Christians include this assurance, but he did not insist on a distinct heartwarming experience or particular consciousness of the Holy Spirit's witness.

In any case Wesley knew from personal experience that the intensity of awareness fades. The feeling of assurance diminishes. But the perception that Christ saves us and the assurance that we are forgiven continue to go hand in hand. Those who thought of faith as a human act and that assurance must be a supernatural intervention by the Holy Spirit pressed Wesley to disconnect the two more radically. An internal witness of the Holy Spirit seemed too extraordinary a phenomenon to be tied so closely to the human act of trusting God and believing God's word. But for Wesley the gift of faith through which Christ saves and the gift of the awareness that one is saved remained closely connected. Both are of the Spirit. Neither is to be understood as an intervention from outside. They constitute decisive moments in the continuous working of grace in our lives.

Randy Maddox provides a fine statement of Wesley's mature conclusions about assurance. Because of the Spirit's inspiration one can "be sensible of Divinely-fostered peace, joy, and love." We do not "perceive the Spirit *per se*, we only perceive the effects of the Spirit's inspiration." The Spirit's witness is "an inward awareness of merciful love that evidences our restored relationship to God. In essence, it is God sharing Godself with us to the point where we can sense Divine mercy and love in a manner analogous to our awareness of our affections and tendencies."[35]

Wesleyans have found it difficult to maintain and continue Wesley's doctrine of assurance. This has been partly because Wesley's own formulations are confused and inconsistent. When Wesley emphasized the warmth of inward feeling or the specialness of the Spirit's witness, he described an experience that is unquestionably a reality for some but one that is not a universal concomitant of Christian faith. When he presents it simply as a fuller expression of justifying faith in general, it does not seem to be needed as a separate doctrine.

Wesley's doctrine of assurance is inseparable from his doctrine of faith. The latter, in exactly the form he developed it, is not convincing today. However, Chapter 3 pointed out that there are current ways of thinking that have striking similarities to Wesley. One of them is provided by process thought. Concerns very much like Wesley's arise in process theology and are dealt with in quite parallel ways.

For process thought, as for Wesley, God's presence (as Holy Spirit) is constitutive of every occasion of human experience. Life, freedom, conscience, peace, joy, and love are among the effects of this presence when the occasions of human experience are open to being formed by it and responsive to it. These effects of the divine, constitutive presence are certainly experienced, and some of them can be consciously noted. In this sense the evidence of the inward working of the Holy Spirit is given equally with, indeed, more fundamentally than, the outward changes that were emphasized by Wesley's critics.

But in most occasions of experience, even among mature Christians, elements of peace, joy, and love are mixed with many other feelings derived from many other sources. If one expects their domination of experience, honest examination will usually lead to disappointment. If one associates such domination with the life of faith, one will doubt that one is a believer. But that peace, joy, and love *can* be pervasively present, and even underlie and make bearable the anxieties and fears and frustrations of life, is attested in the lives of many Christians.

Sometimes the awareness of these inward changes seems to count as assurance for Wesley. But there is a second question that is also highlighted in his reflections. Are we not only aware that peace, joy, and love are present in our lives, but also that they are of God? Do we experience them as evidence of God's forgiving love and transforming power in our lives?

Process theology affirms that in fact they do constitute such evidence. But much that is contributed to our experience from beyond itself does not clearly attest its sources. For example, events in the brain are major contributors to our experience moment by moment, but we can affirm this only through our study of physiological psychology. Even when we accept these theories, our conscious experience does not directly witness to their truth. On the other hand, our feelings are affected by the feelings or mood of those around us. Sometimes we are not aware that our discomfort, for example, is due to an undercurrent of anger on the part of those with whom we are relating. But when this fact is pointed out, we may both be clearer about what we are feeling and also experience that feeling as caused by particular events in our environment. In other words, our conscious experience informed by the theory also confirms it.

The question, now, is what happens in relation to the role of the Holy Spirit in constituting our experience. Obviously, many people who, according to this theory, are benefiting from the work of the Holy Spirit within them do not think of what they find in their experience as coming from the Spirit. If one is persuaded by theoretical considerations that the Spirit is the source, does the experience remain unchanged, giving no support to the theory? Or is the experience clarified and deepened, and does it then also attest to its own origins in God?

Process theology as such is not committed to taking sides on this issue. But I as a Wesleyan process theologian am persuaded that accepting the theory does affect the experience, clarifying and deepening it. I am persuaded also that the clarified and deepened experience does attest to its origins beyond itself, that it is felt as grace, that it does function as a witness to the operations of the Holy Spirit.

Many people who believe in God do so because their experience immediately supports that belief. Sometimes this is a matter of occasional, very special experiences. Sometimes it is a matter of pervasive experience. More often there is some mutual reinforcement between the two. Both are interconnected with beliefs, and when beliefs that provide a different, nontheistic, explanation of experience become convincing, this has an effect upon the experiences themselves. Where the cultural climate becomes uncongenial to theistic explanations, theistic experience itself declines. But this does not mean that these experiences are simply generated by the theistic belief. They provide their own measure of influence upon beliefs. There are many who believe because of experience even though they have difficulty maintaining the beliefs in the face of cultural rejection.

"Assurance" may not today be the best term to give to the immediate experience of the inward working of the Spirit. It may be laden with too much questionable history. But the experience of peace, joy, and love as grace is indeed reassuring, and belief in God's love that is in no way supported by such inward experience is certainly impoverished. Wesley was not wrong to emphasize its desirability and importance and to encourage his followers to expect it. We need to recover the ability to articulate a similar doctrine in the ordinary life of contemporary United Methodism.

CHAPTER 5

The Way of Salvation, II: God's Transformative Work

The New Birth

In the summary of the way of salvation quoted near the beginning of Chapter 4, Wesley spoke of justification and the new birth. Regeneration, or the new birth, is the first moment of sanctification, a moment that occurs simultaneously with justification. From that moment on there is a process of sanctification, the process that characterizes the whole of the Christian life. Justification is a changed relation to God; the new birth is the beginning of that process in which grace, now sanctifying grace, strengthens love for God and for neighbor. The new birth, according to Wesley, is

> that great change which God works in the soul when he brings it into life: when he raises it from the death of sin to the life of righteousness. It is the change wrought in the whole soul by the almighty Spirit of God when it is 'created anew in Christ Jesus,' when it is 'renewed after the image of God', 'in righteousness and true holiness,' when the love of the world is changed into the love of God, pride into humility, passion into meekness; hatred, envy, malice into a sincere, tender, disinterested love for all mankind.[1]

Wesley pressed vigorously the analogy between the natural birth and the spiritual one. He did so especially with reference to his doctrine of spiritual perception. Before their physical birth human beings have sense organs, but they do not see or hear. At birth, instantaneously, or in a very brief time, their senses begin to function. The infant has an entirely new way of being in the world. Similarly,

> while a man is in a mere natural state, before he is born of God, he has, in a spiritual sense, eyes and sees not; a thick impenetrable veil lies upon them. He has ears, but hears not; he is utterly deaf to what he is most of all concerned to hear. . . . Hence he has no knowledge of God, no intercourse with him; . . . But as soon as he is born of

God there is a total change in all these particulars. The 'eyes of his understanding are opened.'[2]

Wesley's typically extravagant language makes it difficult to reconcile what he says on one topic with what he says on others. Here, for example, he speaks so emphatically of the contrast between the condition before and after the new birth that it is hard to see what had been accomplished by prevenient and convicting grace. Surely the spiritual senses had some glimmerings of sight and hearing in order that repentance could take place at all! On the other side, the condition resulting immediately from the new birth sounds so perfect that it is hard to see what more sanctification could accomplish.

On these points, Wesley's account in "The Scripture Way of Salvation" is clearer. There he stated that prevenient grace is responsible for

all the 'drawings' of 'the Father,' the desires after God, which if we yield to them, increase more and more; all that 'light' wherewith the Son of God 'enlighteneth everyone that cometh into the world,' *showing* every man 'to do justly, to love mercy, and to walk humbly with his God,' all the *convictions* which his Spirit from time to time works in every child of man.[3]

These convictions are presumably the convincing grace that brings about repentance. Hence grace has accomplished much before justification and new birth occur. On the other side, Wesley warns passionately against the illusion of new believers that new birth expels all sin:

It is seldom long before they are undeceived, finding sin was only suspended, not destroyed. . . . They now feel two principles in themselves, plainly contrary to each other: 'the flesh lusting against the spirit', nature opposing the grace of God. . . . They feel in themselves, sometimes pride or self-will, frequently *stirring* in their heart, though not *conquering*.[4]

The actual result of the new birth then seems to be that the perception of spiritual reality which had only flickered before becomes established and what is seen is truly recognized and affirmed. This establishes the love of God and neighbor as the real basis of the new life. But the unregenerate nature, with all of its perceptions and habits, is far from obliterated. It resists the newly dominant love.

Wesley's account of the way of salvation gives the impression that justification and new birth occur at a particular time and place.

They constitute so decisive a discontinuity in the course of the work of grace that one would expect the event to stand out in the consciousness and memory of the believer. This was the case for most of the early Methodists, and Wesley had the actual experience of his people very much in mind. On the American frontier also, where so much of the ethos of American Methodism was shaped, this model of dramatic conversion was eminently appropriate.

However, although there must be a beginning to the Christian life, understood as the coming to dominance of the power of love, it is not essential that this be a dramatic event or one that can be singled out in the memory of the Christian. Wesley himself illustrates this. There were times when he identified his Aldersgate experience as that of justification and new birth. But as time passed he acknowledged the judgment of his friends that he had been a Christian long before Aldersgate. Brought up in a devout home and internalizing its Christian piety, he could not say when he first entered the Christian life. The Wesleyan tradition is open both to those who are consciously converted to Christianity from a life of egregious sin or from legalism and to those who have been nurtured into the faith in Christian homes. As George Morris has said very aptly, "Some people walk the Damascus Road; others walk the Emmaus Road."[5]

That Wesley himself was not committed to dramatic conversion as the only entry into Christian life is also clear from his doctrine of baptism. He grew up as an orthodox Anglican affirming baptismal regeneration. His church taught that baptism removed the guilt and power of original sin from the infant and initiated the infant into the Christian life. This doctrine belongs in a far less experiential context than that of Wesley's theology, but Wesley was reluctant to give it up. It underlay his own commitment to infant baptism.

It is true that Wesley saw that many who were baptized, and on that basis claimed to be born again, did not live Christian lives. For them to claim their baptism as grounds for security of salvation deeply offended him. He was forced to distinguish, much more sharply than Anglican doctrine, baptism as an outward sign from the regeneration it signified. But he continued to believe that the infant was freed from original sin when baptized. Few would assert that he ever came to a clear or adequate doctrine.[6]

The objectivism that thus clouded his doctrine of regeneration has played little role in the Wesleyan movement. Infant baptism is accepted as an ingrafting into the church where the inward working of the Spirit is aided through the life of the community of faith. In usual Wesleyan thought, for those baptized in infancy the new birth is temporally connected more with the decision to join the church rather than with baptism as such. At this point youths or adults take responsibility for their own Christian lives, confirming the vows made for them at their baptism. But this does not require a dramatic experience of conversion.

Sanctification

The closest term in the contemporary vocabulary to what Wesley meant by sanctification is spirituality. Many Christians, including many in the Wesleyan churches, feel a hunger for something more than their present participation in Christian life provides them. They understand themselves to be believers, and this status is important to them. They do not feel God's condemnation or condemn themselves. But their lives still seem fragmented, aimless, empty, without sufficient purpose, shallow. They seek some structure or discipline that can respond to these needs. Earlier in this century they would have joined groups for Bible reading and prayer. Many still do. But others find that what occurs in these groups does not meet their needs. Some participate in neo-Wesleyan support groups. Others seek help farther afield, even outside of Christianity.

Wesley agreed that though being a Christian was crucially important, it was not enough. Justification and the new birth initiated Christian life. But the living of that life was much more than simply claiming the status of having been saved at some point in the past. The focus should be on what is happening now. And unless what is happening now is sanctification, it does not suffice.

Some forms of spirituality today focus on moral behavior. More are quests for inner serenity. For Wesley the separation of these two would prevent either from being Christian. His account of sanctification was shaped by both concerns. It was also grounded, as most contemporary forms of spirituality are not, by a careful Biblical and theological analysis. What *is* the defining mark of the regenerate life?

We noticed the crucial issue in the preceding section. It is possible to describe what happens in regeneration in such glowing terms that it seems that sin plays no role in that life. Wesley denied that this is the Biblical account or that it is experientially true. He polemicized against it with special vehemence because he himself had been so attracted to the Moravians among whom this idea was taught. He admired their moral character and their inner serenity. But in the end he did not trust this, and he was convinced that leading Christians to expect moral perfection and serenity as an immediate result of the new birth could only lead to self-deception or despair.

Wesley was equally concerned with an opposite tendency more common among the Protestants of his time. Appealing to Luther's doctrine that we are always both justified and sinful, many could recognize their continuing sinfulness without shame or apology. As long as they believed that God pardoned them, they thought, they could sin without compunction. In their view, salvation was God's business and not theirs. Their personal morality had nothing to do with it. Wesley was appalled by this antinomianism, and his doctrine of sanctification was developed chiefly in opposition to it.

Wesley did not think of his view as novel. He understood it to be that of his church, the Church of England. Nevertheless, it was his most distinctive and widely recognized theological contribution—and it was attacked and praised accordingly. It has done much to shape the ethos of the Wesleyan denominations. Its recovery and adaptation to the contemporary situation in United Methodism is a major burden of this book. We, too, need to find a way between claiming too much and too little for the life-transforming power of grace. We need to have enticing but realistic expectations of what our lives can become. We need to understand our role in the realization of those expectations without supposing that we can bring them about in our own strength. A careful examination of Wesley's teaching can be at least a beginning, if not an extended guide, to our contemporary formulations.

Wesley quoted the teaching of the Church of England as the starting point of his exposition in his sermon, "On Sin in Believers":

> Original sin . . . is the corruption of nature of every man . . . whereby man is . . . in his own nature inclined to evil, so that the flesh lusteth contrary to the Spirit. And this infection of nature doth remain, yea, in them that are regenerated; whereby the lust of the flesh . . . is not subject to the law of God. And although there is no condemnation for them that believe . . . yet this lust hath of itself the nature of sin.[7]

For Wesley it is important to maintain both of the main points made in this doctrine. First, the sinfulness of human nature is not ended by regeneration, so that the Christian life is one of struggling against the continuing presence of sin within the believer. Second, although the continuing lusts are genuinely sinful, believers are not condemned for them by God and should not condemn themselves. The first point is important in preventing false expectations about the Christian life. Its peace and joy are not a function of its relaxed ease in the enjoyment of what God has done for us. But the second point is equally important. Believers are to have peace and joy in the Christian life because they are free from guilt. The continuing presence of sin is not to disturb the enjoyment of reconciliation with God.

Although Wesley accepted this teaching, he interpreted it in light of his conviction that regeneration does effect a crucially significant change. In the new birth the Spirit comes to dominance in the Christian life. The continuing struggle between the Spirit and fallen nature is not an equal one. In the Christian life the fallen nature is not allowed to win. There is no longer sin in the sense of intentionally doing what is wrong. There are powerful sinful impulses, but the Christian does not let them take control. If one who has been a Christian does give control to these impulses, he or she ceases by that act to be a Christian. This insistence that the Christian does not give in to sin is at the heart of Wesley's spirituality.

Because Wesley's own view of what is required by Christian love was so rigorous, his formulation of this teaching is likely to repel us. For example, it seems that not to attend a Methodist meeting when one is able to do so might well constitute a sinful act of the sort that would mean one is no longer a Christian, that one has allowed the sinful nature to rule. On the other hand, since Wesley himself would have been unlikely to draw the extreme conclusion in this instance, another example will serve better. To consider whether we can agree with Wesley's view that when the sinful nature rules we are no longer Christians, we should consider cases that both we and he take more seriously.

Suppose that a Christian learns that an erstwhile friend is spreading lies about her, lies that are extremely damaging. For Wesley the ideal is that the woman should have, as a result of this, nothing but continuing love for this former friend. There would be no defensiveness, no resentment, no anger. But Wesley by no means supposes that as a result of her new birth, the woman will in fact have no such feelings. They are entirely "natural." This does not prevent them from being sinful, and the woman should acknowledge this and seek

God's help in becoming more loving even toward her enemies. But she should not feel guilty or allow the presence of these feelings to reduce her confidence in God's pardon and love.

But suppose the woman responds to this injury by planning to harm the former friend. Suppose she invents stories about him that will be at least as injurious as those that have angered her, and then proceeds to tell these stories to those in position to do the man a great deal of harm. In this case she has given her sinful nature rule. Suppose then that, when confronted about her conduct, she says that she knows she is a sinner but that she counts on the fact that God justifies her all the same, and then continues to spread lies. Would she be at that time a Christian? Wesley's answer was emphatically negative, and we may well agree. She has misunderstood the gospel and is using it to allow her to be a complacent sinner.

The difficult cases lie between the two extremes. Suppose that when the woman learns of the slanders against her she is enraged and tries to turn her informant against the slanderer. Suppose then that she calms down and regrets what she has done even though the anger that motivated it is still there. Would this mean that during the time when her anger was determining what she said she was no longer a Christian?

Wesley did not find this kind of case easy to deal with. He would probably have identified it under the rubric "'sins of surprise': as when one who commonly in patience possesses his soul on a sudden and violent temptation speaks or acts in a manner not consistent with the royal law, 'Thou shalt love thy neighbor as thyself.'"[8] For Wesley the question is the concurrence of the will. To whatever extent one's outburst is voluntary, there is condemnation. To whatever extent it is not, there is none. This answer suggests that the question of whether one is a Christian in the midst of this expression of anger is one of degree. This is quite sensible in itself, but it is difficult to reconcile with Wesley's usual either/or thinking on this matter.

There is a more serious problem. Wesley's treatment of sins of surprise brings to the fore the rigorism that is offensive to most of us. His recognition that the upsurge and dominance of negative emotions may be involuntary is an important concession, and his recognition that the acquiescence of the will is a matter of degree is realistic. But he proceeds from this point to track down the element of the voluntary so as to minimize the excuse that surprise may provide: "There may be some sins of surprise which bring much guilt and condemnation. For in some instances our being surprised is owing to some wilful and culpable neglect; or to a sleepiness of soul which might have been prevented, or shaken off before the temptation came."[9] The implication is clear. One is free from guilt only if one has been continuously alert and maintained full voluntary control of feeling and action whenever that is possible. A relaxed acceptance of events as they come seems always to be culpable in Wesley's view.

The systematic problem arises because Wesley asserted that once we are born again we abstain from all the works of the flesh.[10] Although his list of examples is composed in general of rather gross sins, Wesley's definition of sin implies that *any* wilful transgression, however subtle and excusable, classifies as a work of the flesh. And he says the Christian cannot be engaged in "now transgressing the commandments of God."[11] When he includes failure to act when it is possible as one such transgression, the conclusions are disastrous. This rigorous moral life, in which the will retains control almost always, may well be one valid form of Christian living, but surely it is not the only one. Christian love of God and neighbor may often flourish more where the life of feeling is given freer reign. No doubt sins of surprise will be more frequent in this style of life. But the final result may be superior.

Nevertheless, it would be wrong to suppose that Wesley's purpose was to track down the sinful element in the actions of Christians so as to make them feel guilty. He employed that strategy in relation to those who were unregenerate, in order to bring them to repentance. But it is not appropriate for Christians. On the contrary, they are to be encouraged to believe that they are *not* condemned. Scrupulosity is an impediment to Christian life.

Furthermore, it is not Wesley's actual view that all who have been born again are free from voluntarily transgressing the commandment of love. He seems to have felt that it should be that way, but he was too accurate an observer of what actually transpired to hold consistently to such an extreme position. His sermon on "The Repentance of Believers" makes this clear. Although most of his account is of how sinful dispositions continue after regeneration to affect all that believers do without controlling their actions, he also recognized that the sin that remained present in their lives sometimes did control behavior: "Indeed it is to be feared that many of our words are more than mixed with sin, that they are sinful altogether. For such undoubtedly is all *uncharitable conversation*, all which does not spring from brotherly love, . . . Now how few are there, even among believers, who are in no degree guilty of this?"[12] Again, "Are there not many of their actions which they themselves know are not 'to the glory of God'? Many wherein they did not even aim at this, which were not undertaken with an eye to God?"[13] And finally, "Do they not know a thousand instances wherein they might have done good, to enemies, to strangers, to their brethren, either with regard to their bodies or their souls, and they did it not?"[14]

This analysis is of Christians who were regenerate. Some of their "sinful" acts of commission and omission may not have been voluntary, but Wesley was not excusing believers here on this basis. Believers "knew" that their actions were not to the glory of God, that they did "not even aim at this." Wesley's comment about sins of omission follows immediately on his quotation of James 4:17: "To him that knoweth to do good and doth it not, to him it is sin" (KJV). It seems clear that Wesley recognized that believers *do* sometimes, even frequently, allow motives other than love to control their behavior. Yet there is no suggestion here that in the moment they commit these presumably voluntary sins they lose their status as justified and born again.

The actual bases on which Wesley judged whether one remains a Christian were far less rigorous than they sometimes seem. Without violating his intentions, we might propose that when one is born again one enters a life in which one's purpose is that all that one do and say be according to the law of love. This excludes acts of gross immorality. It also means that one does not persist in avoidable actions that are clearly wrong. But sin still pervasively influences even the best actions of believers, and it may sometimes be determinative of what the Christian does. On the other hand, as Christians become aware of this continuing power of sin, they acknowledge it and seek God's aid in struggling against it. If they deny it to themselves and others and refuse to seek God's help against it, they cease to be responsibly Christian.

This understanding of the Christian life is still a demanding one that would exclude many who participate regularly in the life of the church. It provides a significant basis for self-examination and for mutual encouragement and support in Christian growth. It gives direction to a Wesleyan spirituality that is close to Wesley's own.

Wesley saw that some who for a time seemed very serious about their Christian life nevertheless acted in ways incompatible with it.

He did not claim to know for sure that they had ever been authentic Christians, but he was certain that they were not that now. And he left open the possibility that at an earlier point their faith had been genuine. He described this as falling from grace, and Wesleyans have often called it "backsliding."

This seems to correspond with lived experience today. For example, there may be a man who for some time tries seriously and with apparent success to bring his life into accord with the law of love. Then something happens. Someone injures him. His response is not simply a rage that occasionally takes over. It is, instead, a settled commitment to vengeance. Here is an area of life in which he has decided not to allow love to have its way. It is reasonable to judge that he has ceased to be a Christian even though he continues to attend church and to behave as a Christian in other ways. He can only become an authentic Christian again through acknowledging the depth of his sin and renewing his faith in God's pardon.

Today we must reflect on reasons for people to cease to identify themselves as Christians other than their falling into the grip of sin. Not to do so would be to fail to recognize the difference between Wesley's situation and ours. But even in his day there were some unbelievers whose rejection of Christianity was not based on unwillingness to submit to the law of love. Some rejected it because they found Christian teachings incredible. Wesley tried to accommodate his message to them by relativizing those features of traditional doctrine that were most troublesome and explaining others in reasonable and understandable ways. But not all were convinced. Others rejected Christianity because they judged it to breed intolerance, self-righteousness, credulity, and other forms of evil. Wesley responded by showing that the gospel, rightly understood, did none of these things. But again, not all were convinced. These people may have been genuine Christians at one time, but their departure from the faith should not be thought of as backsliding.

In our time many reject Christianity because they judge that its teachings lead to psychologically unhealthy states, or because it supports an unjust and destructive patriarchy, or because it fails to deal with the most urgent issues of our time, or because it is vapid and boring. Others leave Christianity because they are converted to another religious community, such as Buddhism or Islam. A Wesleyan response today is to try to reformulate the gospel in light of the valid objections raised against it, so that these do not continue to justify the rejection of Christianity as a whole. Wesleyans may also incorporate what is good in those traditions to which people go so that they will not need to leave the church in order to find these values. But thus far we have not responded in our time as effectively as Wesley did in his. Many remain unconvinced.

There are, therefore, many other ways of rejecting Christian faith besides backsliding. "Backsliding" remains a useful category for understanding real events, but it must not be used as a way of describing all rejections of Christianity. Before judging harshly those who leave, we need to examine carefully those failures on our part that led them to their decision.

Perfect Love

Wesley's depiction of authentic Christian life in terms of its severe demands was partly motivated by his honesty. He saw it that way. But it was also motivated by his strong desire to encourage Christians to seek more. The life of basically successful struggle against sin is far superior to the bondage to sin that is the natural condition of human beings, or the bondage to the law that constitutes an intermediate state. But it does not embody all that may be hoped for—all that is promised in the Bible. Just as by contrasting the Christian life with ordinary life Wesley tried to bring people to repentance and justifying faith; so by contrasting the fullness of what the Bible promises with the actuality of ordinary Christian life Wesley pressed Christians to expect and strive for more. It was when he was calling Christians to this hope and effort that he spoke most harshly of how they live. But this harsh language was accompanied by glowing words about the possibility of what could be.

Wesley sometimes spoke of this as entire sanctification. By that he meant that it completes the process begun with the new birth. In the new birth the Spirit assumes dominance in the believer. In entire sanctification the Spirit removes the root of sin, that is, all in the believer that has continued to resist God. The life initiated by the new birth is one of victorious struggle, but a painful and disturbing one all the same. The consummation of that struggle in entire sanctification is the end of that struggle through the disappearance of the enemy.

Wesley had strongly opposed the Moravians who saw this final victory as won already in the new birth. But he was not unmoved by their quotations from scripture or by their vision of the Christian life. Instead, he applied all this to the ultimate goal of that life, a goal toward which all Christians should look and which, he was convinced, some attained.

The content of this goal follows from all that has been said about the Christian life. In ordinary Christian life, love of God and neighbor struggle with other feelings. By the power of the Spirit Christians can make their actions conform to this love. But this involves a painful suppression of other desires that have not conformed to the law of love. Now in entire sanctification love has its way. One genuinely loves God with *all* one's heart, mind, soul, and strength. There are no competing motives. Hence one's actions flow directly from love. The time of strenuous self-discipline and effortful striving is over. One has attained perfect love.

This is not a matter of human achievement. Wesley repudiated that view entirely. On the other hand, he did not believe that God simply does what God wants with people apart from their wills. Chapter 2 considered the way in which God's Spirit works in all people, liberating and empowering and transforming them, but only in and through their own personal decision and acting. Apart from grace one can do no good at all. But grace can work effectively within one only as one recognizes one's need and allows it to do so.

At every point grace is primary. It is convincing or convicting grace that makes one aware of one's continuing needs and of one's helplessness to satisfy them apart from grace. The external means of grace, such as preaching, can work with the internal activity of grace to make this occur. But it does not occur apart from the willing of the one in whom it happens, a willing that is itself the work of grace. Grace also works within one to strengthen love and to weaken the power of sin. Here again it does so only as personal willing allows, a willing that is also the work of grace. Thus entire sanctification is a work of grace.

The strong sense of the priority of grace in sanctification sang its way into the Methodist soul through hymns, of which there is no finer example than the concluding verse of "Love Divine, All Loves Excelling," which is worth quoting again here:

> Finish then thy new creation,
> Pure and spotless let us be;
> Let us see thy great salvation
> Perfectly restored in thee;

Changed from glory into glory,
Till in heaven we take our place,
Till we cast our crowns before thee,
Lost in wonder, love, and praise.[15]

Entire sanctification is also an effect of faith. Just as there is no justification apart from faith, so there is no sanctification without it. The inner working of grace opens the spiritual eyes of believers to the outer working of Christ. It is as they lay hold of that work and claim its fuller benefits for themselves that sanctification occurs within them.

Nowhere in this process is there any basis for boasting. Indeed, any tendency to boast is a clear indication that one has hardly begun the process of sanctification! Such boasting cannot express perfect love. In any case, of what is the sanctified person to boast? Of Christ's mercy? Of the effective work of the Holy Spirit? If so, there is nothing wrong with "boasting." But this "boasting" is simply the praise of God. The problem is that a man who praises God for the wonderful things God is doing in *him*, may not be free from an interest in having it noticed that it is indeed in *him*. Too easily this can be self-righteousness parading as praise of God.

Wesley was aware of this danger, and he did what he could to reduce it. But this did not cause him to abandon his emphasis on perfect love. Far worse than this risk, he was convinced, was depicting the Christian life in such a way that believers would rest content with the struggles that characterize its early stages or, worse, decide that a bit of sinning was acceptable as long as one could rely on God's pardon.

Wesley believed the movement toward perfect love could take one of two forms. It could be a gradual growth in grace. Step by step, bit by bit, the Christian might form habits that weakened sinful motivations. Some of the powerful desires of ambition, greed, and lust may subside. Tendencies to rage may decline. Love could have its way with less struggle, eventually with none at all.

If Wesley had limited himself to this vision of growth in grace, some of the problems that his doctrine of perfection raised would have been less severe. But he took another step. The analogy he saw between the new birth and entire sanctification led him to speak also of a second dramatic blessing. Perfect love might come about instantaneously. Even this doctrine would have done little harm if this had been presented simply as a possibility, something that God might, for God's own reasons, occasionally do. But here Wesley took another step that had so many negative consequences that much of the Wesleyan movement abandoned, to its loss, the entire doctrine of perfection.

In "The Repentance of Believers," after quoting Biblical texts that he believed referred to entire sanctification, Wesley wrote:

> You have therefore good reason to believe he is not only able but *willing* to do this—to 'cleanse you from all your filthiness of flesh and spirit', to 'save you from all your uncleannesses'. This is the thing which you now long for: this is the faith which you now particularly need, namely, that the great physician, the lover of my soul, is willing to 'make me clean'. But is he willing to do this tomorrow or today? Let him answer for himself: 'Today, if ye will hear my voice, harden not your hearts.' If you put it off till tomorrow, you 'harden your hearts'; you refuse to 'hear his voice'. Believe therefore that he is willing to save you *today*. He is willing to save you *now*. Behold, 'now is the accepted time.' He now saith, 'Be thou clean!' Only believe; and you also will immediately find, 'All things are possible to him that believeth.'[16]

Wesley is here exhorting his hearers to think that, if only they will believe that God will remove all motives other than love from their souls, God will in fact do so. This invites intense feelings that no doubt have dramatic effects in believers. But the result is rarely, if ever, what is promised. The result may be that one *believes* that she or he has been made perfect. Then the need to hold onto this belief against countervailing evidence is intense and leads to self-deception. Either one conceals impure motives from one's own notice or one supposes that, after all, they must not be impure, since God has allowed them to remain. The intensely honest self-examination in which Wesley was so gifted is likely to decline among those convinced they are entirely sanctified.

Furthermore, the self-righteousness which does not appear in the one who is truly loving can hardly help but appear here among those who believe themselves to be entirely sanctified. If one has an intense experience that one honestly thinks is the second blessing which Wesley promised to all who believe, one will testify to this. Of course, one will say, sincerely, that it is a gift. But only a few in the crowd have received the gift that Wesley has promised to all who believe. That means the others do not believe. The difference is palpable. The one who thinks she or he has received the gift truly believes; the others do not. The recipient has successfully met the condition that the others have failed to meet. But Wesley told them that God willed to give the blessing to all! How can the few who have supposedly received it fail to see themselves as superior? How can the others fail to feel despair and guilt?

Wesley's own later teaching softened these dangers. The danger arises especially when one supposes that entire sanctification is a state into which one enters, a state in which the basis of sin has been completely uprooted. If in that state the power of sinful nature is gone, then it would seem that nothing could overcome the perfection in love that has been attained. Accordingly, once one has received the second blessing one would expect forevermore to be entirely sanctified.

Wesley recognized that this did not happen. People who had experienced entire sanctification sometimes fell from that state, and some of these subsequently recovered it:

> Some years since, I was inclined to think that one who had once enjoyed and lost the pure love of God must never look to enjoy it again till they were just stepping into eternity. But experience has taught us better things. We have now numerous instances of those who had cast away that unspeakable blessing and now enjoy it in a larger measure than ever.[17]

Here entire sanctification is depicted not as a continuing state but as a matter of moment-by-moment life. Interpreted in this way his sermon would not have significant negative consequences. One would be asking God, moment by moment, to give one purity of love in that moment.

It is doubtful that all of Wesley's remarks about entire sanctification can be interpreted in this way. Indeed, his most careful response to his critics moved in a quite different direction. There it seems that only those whose experience of the second blessing bears permanent fruit can be believed. In considering the evidence by which one may judge one's own experience, Wesley wrote: "Not that the feeling all love and no sin is a sufficient proof. Several have experienced this for a considerable time and yet were afterwards convinced that their souls were not entirely renewed and that sin was only laid asleep, not destroyed."[18]

Yet in other equally central sources Wesley explained that entire sanctification does not do away with the possibility of competing interests. Near the outset of his sermon, "Christian Perfection," he stressed that this condition does not make one free from temptation. This suggests that the disappearance of corrupt nature is either not complete or not permanent. "There are children of God who . . . for the present feel no temptation. . . . But this state will not last always."[19] Furthermore, the attaining of Christian perfection did not mean that there is no further growth possible. "However much soever any man hath attained, or in how high a degree soever he is perfect, he hath still need to 'grow in grace', and daily to advance in the knowledge and love of God his saviour."[20]

Wesley's doctrine of entire sanctification was accompanied by an extension of his doctrine of assurance. Generally the assurance that is given by the Holy Spirit is that the believer is pardoned by God and is therefore a child of God. But Wesley taught that the new gift of the Spirit, perfection in love, was also accompanied by the assurance that this work had been accomplished. As in the case of justification, "we know it by the witness and by the fruit of the Spirit. And, first, by the witness. As when we were justified the Spirit bore witness with our spirit that our sins were forgiven; so, when we were sanctified, he bore witness that they were taken away."[21]

Whether Wesley had a consistent position on perfection is hard to say, and even if he did, it is doubtful that it could be transposed unchanged into our own time. But we *can* say that in the United Methodist churches today it would be very valuable to renew the goal of perfect love, recognizing with Wesley that it is the work of grace in those who believe. The meaning of love would need to be carefully formulated to avoid the exaggerations to which Wesley was rhetorically prone. We would have to pay much more careful attention to unconscious motivations and causes than did he.

It is quite possible and desirable to ask ourselves how much we really care what happens to others and in the wider world, when these events neither hurt nor benefit us in any obvious way. We can then go on to ask how we feel toward those whose words and actions are, in our best judgment, objectively unjust and injurious? Can we disagree and oppose their actions while genuinely caring for them as human beings? To what extent are our actions controlled or influenced by our love?

We can also ask about our attitudes toward those with whom we find ourselves in competition, or those who threaten or malign us, or those whose company we find particularly unpleasant. Do we genuinely want the best for these people, too? Do we feel empathy for them even when we dislike them? What other feelings do we have toward them? On which feelings do we act?

We cannot always be accurate in such self-analysis. Most of us can get further in self-understanding by working in groups, allowing others to check and challenge what we say against other indications of the reality of our feelings and their power. Also there are many other questions to be asked. The most complex analyses are required for those to whom we are closest, those whom we most naturally claim to love. None of this is easy, but examining ourselves with respect to how much we love one another can provide a realistic indication of how far God's sanctifying grace has brought us and of where further it would lead us.

More difficult and problematic is the analysis of love for God. As noted in Chapter 3, Wesley distinguished this too sharply from love for neighbor. Today we should begin with the neighbor. If we do not love the neighbor, we deceive ourselves if we think we love God. But to love God extends the range of our love. To love God is to love all God's creatures, not only the human ones. To love God is also to seek to discern what God is doing in the world and to give ourselves to working with that. In particular, it is to discern the work of grace within ourselves and to celebrate it. It is both to intensify our concern for what happens in the world, because all that happens affects God, and also, finally, to relativize it, believing that in God it is ultimately saved whatever we do. And it may include some effort to discern what feelings our awareness of God and of God's work generates in us, asking whether these feelings can be called love.

From day to day and from year to year love can become a stronger force in our lives. We can work and pray for the weakening of those other forces that limit and derail it. We will not let hope lead us to become less realistic and honest in discerning the reality. Recognizing the power of resentment and defensiveness, envy and greed, longing for security and desire for praise is far better than pretending they are weaker than they are. Repressing hostile feelings, or simply trying to will them away, does not weaken them. Acting on norms that are too far from our feelings can be counterproductive.

But none of this means that the goal of perfect love misdirects our energies. Nor does it mean that there is any necessary limit to the approximation to that goal that the Holy Spirit can work in us.

There are people whose concern for the wellbeing of others is largely disinterested and who extend that concern even toward those whom they emotionally dislike. In some cases the disliking also fades as love leads to understanding. We need not be cynical about the possibility of perfect love. But we should rejoice in whatever love we actually find within us, not feeling guilty because it falls so far short of perfection. Confidence that God works love in our hearts through the Holy Spirit strengthens and encourages us. But we should not expect that intensity of belief that God will do whatever we ask will be the major contributor to the emergence of greater love within us.

There is no guarantee that growth in grace along these lines always leads toward right action. As Wesley emphasized repeatedly, love does not guarantee knowledge or understanding. Actions done in love may be objectively harmful. That believers may not act well is not only because of ordinary ignorance. There may be basic honest disagreement as to what actions properly express love. Some will suppose that love of neighbor precludes participating in actions, such as war, that may lead to the neighbor's death. Others see just war theory as more accurately explaining what love requires. Some believe that Christian love accepts the context of contemporary society and seeks to minister to those who suffer within it. Others are convinced that only efforts to change the context reflect real understanding of the needs of the neighbor. We will return to questions of this sort in Chapter 6.

CHAPTER 6

The Role of Law

The Importance of the Law

The law was of great importance for all the major Reformers. The argument of the early Reformers was against the role it played in Roman Catholic teaching. It served there in such a way as to deny that justification is by grace alone through faith. That is, some measure of righteousness as obedience to law was seen as a condition of justification.

Luther attributed two crucial roles to the law. First, it is a teacher and disciplinarian in the wider society. Children are to be brought up in obedience to the law. It is the basis of social order. Second, it brings about the recognition of each person's participation in universal sinfulness. To appreciate the full demand of God is at once to recognize one's total inability to fulfil that demand. Hence one is ready to throw oneself on the mercy of God and to trust in Christ's saving work rather than in any merit of one's own.

A third use of the law was widely accepted by Protestants. This was as a norm and guide for the Christian life. Luther himself resisted this. That life, in his view, is to be lived by faith alone. Of course, to live by faith is to be obedient to the one in whom one places one's confidence. Luther was not antinomian. But for him the nature of Christian life is not moral striving to conform to God's law. It is the free expression of the love that arises from faith.

Calvin was far more committed to this third use of the law. Luther's rejection of the law as governing Christian life was accompanied by an acceptance of the reality that the public spheres of politics and economics are not governed by Biblical principles. This was the famous Two Kingdom theory. Calvin, in contrast, wanted the whole of the social order Christianized. The story of Calvinist efforts to apply the teaching of the Bible to civil governance in Geneva, in Scotland, and in Massachusetts is well known.

There were several problems with the effort to bring all society under the Christian law. One was that, in adapting it to actual social conditions, compromise, whether acknowledged or not, was inevitable and actual. To identify one important example, society had to use forms of coercion that were in tension with the gospel. A second was that even in this compromised form, the Christian law as understood by some had to be imposed on others who understood it differently as well as on those who rejected it altogether. For the sake of social order the Christian state had to restrict the freedom of those who dissented. This pressure led, in the extreme case, to the execution of Servetus. Third, and most important, the close connection between true belief and social order contributed to the religious wars that wracked Europe, especially in the first half of the seventeenth century.

The differences among the Reformation churches and their shared difference with Roman Catholicism survived these wars. It provided part of the context of Wesley's work. But the situation he faced was, nevertheless, profoundly changed. We will consider three elements in his situation and then discuss his response in reverse order.

(1) The major reaction to the religious wars was a move to toleration. This was partly an ideal that arose among those less committed to Christianity or who rejected it altogether. For the sake of peace and harmony they wanted to shift loyalty from church to state, forcing the religious bodies to live together in peace. This would also mean that religious commitments would not cause nations to go to war with one another. But the ideal of tolerance also emerged within Christianity itself, especially among those who were persecuted, but increasingly among those who saw the contradiction between the gospel message and the way Christians were killing one another over different interpretations and applications.

By Wesley's time some political toleration of diverse religious groups was taken for granted. England understood itself to be a Christian nation, and it expressed this commitment through the establishment of the Church of England. But the Church of England was expected to tolerate considerable diversity within its life, and some freedom for dissenters was affirmed. Hardly anyone wanted to apply the law to public life after the fashion of the earlier Calvinists. In this sense Luther's Two Kingdom view had gained the practical, if unacknowledged, victory.

(2) The shared commitment to tolerance was connected with a

heightened appreciation of reason. Although the earlier Reformers had never identified faith with right belief, the importance of accurate theology in order to protect faith from distortions had led to a very close connection between justifying faith and correct beliefs, especially in Protestant Scholasticism. The arguments for one or another view of what beliefs are correct rested on the authority of the Bible. To many, some of the resultant doctrines appeared highly unreasonable. It seemed even more unreasonable to demand their acceptance on purely authoritarian grounds. More and more people came to believe that reason was a better guide.

The appeal to reason against authoritarianism could be a weapon of enemies of Christianity against the churches. But the importance of reason, like tolerance, was widely accepted among Christians. Most Christians claimed that their beliefs, including their belief in Biblical authority, were reasonable. The tone of theological argument was thus markedly changed.

The rationalistic spirit tended to moderate the understanding of the requirements of the Gospel. Common-sense virtue was substituted for Biblical teaching by some and read into the Bible by others. At the same time the sharp juxtaposition of grace to works was moderated. Reasonable beliefs and reasonable morality came to be regarded as the conditions or marks of justification. The need for grace became less apparent and ceased to be emphasized. For many, the sharp profile of justification by grace through faith alone disappeared even when the language was retained.

(3) On the other side, some of the most intense and devoted Christian believers strongly emphasized grace and its transforming power. For them, this was the gospel. It is grace alone through faith that works salvation, and this salvation is from the power of sin. There is no need for the third use of the law, since grace is the power of the new life. Grace determines the form that it takes.

It was in this context that Wesley renewed the teaching of the law. The situation was very different from that of the earlier Reformers for whom the primary context was Roman Catholicism. This was not the case for Wesley. Even when he was renewing the doctrine of justification by grace through faith alone, it was not Catholic teaching against which he formulated his own rejection of works as a condition of justification. Similarly, he was not influenced by reaction against Roman Catholic teaching in his treatment of the law. Hence, in seeing what is distinctive of Wesley, it is important to understand

117

his treatment of law and gospel in this new context. We will consider his position in relation to the three elements of his context described above, but in reverse order.

(1) Although he was drawn to the spirit of those, especially the Moravians, who depreciated the law, he was convinced that they were wrong in doing so. Their teaching assumed that the power of sin was truly broken by grace through justifying faith. But Wesley, as we have seen, was convinced that it was not. He saw many evidences of the continuing power of sin, a power against which the believer must struggle constantly. A relaxed confidence in God's power would not do. The law is of urgent importance for Christian life.

Of course, it is possible to believe that sin remains in the believer and to acknowledge that moral guidelines for Christian living are needed and yet to argue that what the believer needs to hear is the gospel and not the law. There were those in Wesley's day who argued precisely this. Some of his own preachers claimed to preach only Christ and the gospel, accusing the others, including Wesley, of being "legal preachers." They believed that it is the positive message of the gospel that draws sinners to Christ and that it is the continuing preaching of the gospel that feeds their souls. Hence, for them, the law had little place.

This provoked Wesley to explicit reflection about the role of the law in "Of Preaching Christ."[1] There he asserted that in all preaching there should be both law and gospel, although the balance may vary according to the situation of the hearer. When the hearers do not have faith, the main emphasis should be on the law in order to bring them to repentance. With those who are new Christians, the emphasis is on the gospel. As they move more deeply into the Christian life the preaching of the law becomes important again. But its function is different, and therefore the presentation of the law will be different:

> But when these grow in grace and in the knowledge of Christ, a wise builder would preach the law to them again, only taking particular care to place every part of it in a gospel light as not only a command but a privilege also, as a branch of the glorious liberty of the sons of God. He would take equal care to remind them that this is not the cause but the fruit of their acceptance with God; . . . and that all true obedience springs from love to him. . . . To those who were careless or drawing back he would preach it in another manner, nearly as he did before they were convinced of sin. To

those meanwhile who were earnest but feebleminded, he would preach the gospel chiefly, yet variously intermixing more or less of the law according to their various necessities.[2]

This discussion of diversity within the third use of the law is a distinctive contribution of Wesley. But in this context he did not thematize what is no doubt his most distinctive teaching. For actually Wesley introduced a fourth use of the law. As described in the preceding chapter, Wesley also preached the law to believers in order to convince them that their lives fall far short of what they might be if they would accept God's second blessing. This is highly analogous to the second use of the law, differing only in that it emphasizes that those who hear it are not condemned, that they are already children of God.[3]

(2) The law that Wesley would preach to unbeliever and believer alike was not the natural moral law of the rationalists, although he took something like this for granted and occasionally made appeal to it. Neither was it primarily the Ten Commandments, which have played so large a part in giving meaning to "the law" for other theologians, although he certainly accepted their authority. It was the extremely demanding law of the Bible, and in particular the demands of Jesus. "By 'preaching the law'," Wesley stated, "I mean explaining and enforcing the commands of Christ briefly composed in the Sermon on the Mount."[4] That this was indeed his primary understanding of the law is evident in his preaching in general. Of his published sermons, thirteen are entitled "Upon Our Lord's Sermon on the Mount" and many of the remainder are influenced by Jesus' sayings there. It was in the radical teachings of Jesus that Wesley found the understanding of righteousness that brought sinners to repentance and prodded the Christian to ever more diligent efforts.

Wesley summed up the law he found in the Sermon on the Mount under the heading of the law of love. Perfect love of God and neighbor is the all-inclusive requirement. But this by no means implied that only the motive of our action matters, or that pious sentiment can substitute for outward virtue. Wesley spelled out in detail the behavior that follows from love. And this is preached to believers as law, in the sense that they are to act as love requires even when they are inwardly torn by conflicting desires. The life of the justified is marked by acting according to the requirements of love, not waiting until one's motives are pure. Purity of motive comes only with entire sanctification.

(3) Wesley accepted the context of religious tolerance without question. Indeed, as the next chapter will show, he derived from the law strong reasons for minimizing theological differences and maximizing respect for those who differed. His attitude went far beyond the usual toleration. This meant that he did not apply the law to the way in which public affairs are to be ordered by the state. Only rarely does he campaign for government legislation to deal with the social problems that he notes.

Although Wesley does not derive from the law proposals for a system of government or economics, the law is far from privatistic. Privatism is a danger if one emphasizes only the gospel. Wesley's gospel was addressed to the individual soul in its relation to God. If the focus is on faith alone, then this private relation of the individual to God is likely to dominate. But the law is primarily about relations. It commands love, which is inherently relational, and the command of love of neighbor is inherently social. Christian righteousness is spelled out primarily in terms of the way people relate to one another. It is the distortions in these relations against which Wesley chiefly polemicized.

Furthermore, these relations are not viewed sentimentally. To speak of loving the neighbor when one refrains from actual assistance is sentimental slush in which Wesley took no interest. When the neighbor's need is economic, love expresses itself in economic terms. Since Wesley worked chiefly among the poor, and since their economic needs were great, concern for righteousness in the use of money was of major concern to him.

Theodore Jennings has recently shown that Wesley followed the teachings of Jesus closely and therefore advocated an evangelical economics.[5] On the other hand, Wesley did not campaign for governmental reform. He focused primarily on how Christians should understand money theologically and how they should deal with it practically. Because he stayed close to the New Testament in this area, one in which the church as a whole had long since given up the effort to be literally faithful, Wesley's teachings were radical indeed. Furthermore, he was serious about their implementation in his own life and in that of his followers.

Wesley understood Christians to be stewards of all that they have, and unlike many who use this language, he meant it very seriously indeed. In his sermon on "The Good Steward" he put it this way:

> A steward . . . is not at liberty to use what is lodged in his hands as *he* pleases, but as his master pleases. He has no right to dispose of anything which is in his hands, but according to the will of his Lord. . . . Now this is exactly the case of every man with relation to God. . . . And he entrusts us with them [possessions] on this express condition, that we use them only as our Master's goods, and according to the particular directions which he has given us in his Word.[6]

Wesley left his readers in no doubt as to what those directions are. At the final judgment Christ will address us thus:

> In what manner didst thou employ that comprehensive talent, *money?* . . . Not squandering it away in vain expenses, the same as throwing it into the sea? Not hoarding it up to leave behind thee, the same as burying it in the earth? But first supplying thy own reasonable wants, together with those of thy family; then restoring the remainder to me, through the poor, whom I had appointed to receive it; looking upon thyself as only one of that number of poor whose wants were to be supplied out of that part of my substance, which I had placed in thy hands for that purpose.[7]

That this was not idle rhetoric on Wesley's part was indicated by his personal practice. He was in fact a "gentleman," though he would have reacted violently against the title, and he lived as a gentleman throughout his life. He did not give away all his goods, and he did not teach that others should do so. He earned, chiefly from his writings, as much as two thousand pounds a year, a very considerable sum in a time when one of his preachers, married and with two children, might receive about sixty-five pounds.[8] But Wesley lived modestly as a gentleman and gave away most of what he received. At his death he left no estate behind him. He taught that those with families should provide minimally for their needs, and then, unless they could be sure that one of them would follow strict Christian practices in the use of money, "bestow all the rest in such a manner as . . . would be most for the glory of God."[9]

Although Wesley did not translate this law expressing love and governing the Christian life into proposals for legislation, he did not limit his interest in economics to matters of personal virtue. He saw that the misery of the poor was affected by socio-economic forces, and he tried to understand these. His most extended efforts at economic analysis are to be found in his *Thoughts on the Present Scarcity of Provisions*.[10] Few would find this analysis satisfactory today. The point is only that engaging in social analysis and entering into the public debate on this basis was for Wesley a normal and proper expression of his love for those who suffer. The reason he did not urge this on his followers is more likely to be that few of them had the education to take part in such public debates than that he did not see its importance.

The one area in which Wesley *did* engage in political action was in his work against slavery. In an uncharacteristic fashion, his major writing against slavery, *Thoughts on Slavery*,[11] appeals to principles of natural law rather than explicitly to the law of love. Presumably his interest in changing public practice led him to make this more widely accepted appeal. In this book he argues that "not only slaveholders, but also those responsible for unjust legislation must expect God's punishment for their misdeeds."[12] But he did not appeal directly for legislation. Eventually, however, he supported the anti-slavery leaders who took the case to Parliament. He was not opposed to the use of political means to effect ends that were required by the natural law as well as by Christian principles.

Contemporary Disintegration

In Wesley's thinking the gospel was intensely personal. The law showed that the expression of the love it engendered was social. On some occasions, this social aspect took on societal dimensions.

Today the situation has changed. The meaning of "salvation" has been extended as a result of Biblical scholarship, especially on Jesus' proclamation of the Kingdom of God. Jesus' reference was not simply to an inner state of heart religion. It was to a world in which God's will is done. Without questioning that salvation has meaning in personal life, we have come to recognize that it is social as well. The social aspect that Wesley found in the law is also in the gospel.

Nevertheless, it proves difficult to proclaim the Kingdom of God as good news. It was easier during the heyday of the social gospel, when God's working in history could be viewed as progressive victories over evil. Today that is far from clear, and preaching about society has once again become primarily law. Most of this is based on social analysis and hence deals with the societal issues that were at the fringes of Wesley's work.

The reason Wesley did not preach about societal issues may have been that the people to whom he preached could do little about them. They *could* respond to the needs of their neighbors, and Wesley frequently preached about their doing so. But laws were made by other people, and it was those other people who controlled the economy as well. To preach to the poor of England about influencing legislation would have made sense only if one were calling for revolution. And Wesley was politically conservative.

In a changed situation, where the people in the pew are all participants in determining legislation, the law of love calls them to exercise their power for the sake of all. To do so requires analysis of what is going on and proposals for societal reform. Wesleyans in general have recognized this and accepted the need for Christians to participate responsibly in the democratic process. They have believed it appropriate for their denominations to channel their societal concerns and to seek to influence legislation.

However, while we have extended and applied Wesley's understanding of law to societal matters, we have abandoned the teaching of the law almost everywhere else. Some remains with regard to sexual morality, a topic on which Wesley said and wrote remarkably little. Some remains also with regard to our duties to the church. But on the whole a very personal gospel has triumphed over law. The remaining law, that dealing with societal matters, is so disconnected with this intimately personal gospel that it seems to function as an independent focus of Christian concern. The dialectic of law and gospel, so crucial for Wesley, is broken.

As noted above, Wesley wrote on this topic in response to a movement among his preachers to preach the gospel only. Wesley's report on what happened to the societies that had received the gospel preaching is a good predictor of what is happening to us:

> When I came to review the societies, with great expectation of finding a vast increase, I found most of them lessened by one-third, one entirely broken up . . . and of those that remained, the far greater number in every place were cold, weary, heartless and dead.[13]

Wesley goes on to contrast that with the vitality and growth that continued to occur where gospel and law were preached together.

To clarify the difference between our situation and the one favored by Wesley, we can return to the issue of economics. Wesley touched on this in many of his sermons and devoted two exclusively to it. Nowhere in his preaching does he discuss solutions to systemic economic problems, but pervasively he presents his understanding of what the law of love requires of each of us in the management of our resources. The preaching of the law forces the hearer to sustained consideration of the fundamental nature of "property" and of personal expenditures.

Today, despite the overwhelming importance of economics in society and in our personal lives, the topic is rarely treated in sermons at all. There are references to the evils of social injustice, and occasionally these are made real to the hearer in ways that truly function as law. During the "stewardship" campaign some preaching about generosity to the church is to be expected. But that is all. Few preachers would dare to connect their denunciations of social injustice with the lives of their members or to prescribe to them what constitutes a Christian use of resources!

There are three reasons for this withdrawal. The first is that most Christians do not want any interference in their moral lives. They regard these as their private affairs. The second is that few ministers have much confidence as to how Christians should live. Strong statements about social justice may take the place of calls for obedient living because we may be clearer about what changes would improve society than about how we should individually live. The third is that ministers who believe that the Christian should adhere to high standards of morality are not always willing to set the example. The result is an appeal to common-sense morality, more and more vaguely understood—just that appeal against which Wesley reacted so strongly. Even this is used more as reassurance than as law.

In this context, as Wesley understood, the gospel has lost its power. It functions as good news only when the need for it is felt and when it is experienced as meeting that need. These conditions were met in early Methodism. They are not met now. The gospel is now presented chiefly in psychological terms, vaguely related to common-sense morality. Since it responds to no urgent need, it can be quietly believed and accepted with little effect. Those with urgent psychological needs go elsewhere to deal with them. The decline in membership and in the enthusiasm of those who remain continues.

Wesleyan Renewal

We talk much in United Methodism about reversing our decline. Too often we suppose we can do this by studying "successful" churches and emulating them or by organizing ourselves to be more "evangelistic" in the sense of working harder to get more members. There is nothing Wesleyan about *this* kind of pragmatism. Wesley was interested in results, but he measured these by the attainment of scriptural holiness. Furthermore, he knew what he meant by that, and he could explain it in a way that made possible useful judgments about progress and regress.

Another strategy for renewal is "returning to Wesley." Those who advocate this have varied notions of what this might entail. It turns out that virtually all such proposals are in fact highly selective. Conservative evangelicals want the church to return to the Wesley of one book who preached powerful revivals and taught strict personal morality. High church Methodists want to return to the faithful priest of the Church of England who went daily to communion and retained a high ecclesiology to his death. Liberationist Methodists want to return to the Wesley who devoted his life to the poor and denounced the rich. Liberal Methodists want to return to the Wesley who polemicized against predestination and qualified natural depravity in order to affirm individual freedom and responsibility. Psychologistic Methodists want to return to the Wesley who emphasized actual religious experience and the importance of mutual openness in small groups.

All those Wesleys exist. But of course they are also all abstractions from the historical reality. Each picture is a tendentious interpretation of selections from the data. This is as true of mine as of others. We tend to claim too much for our pictures in order to justify our prejudices from them. That is why I have in the past been wary of seeking renewal in this way.

However, at another level we can and should return to Wesley. We need to analyze our situation and the reasons for our decline as tough-mindedly as he analyzed the conditions of his own time. We need to become as clear about our goals as he was about his. And we need to strategize as realistically as he to achieve them.

Our goals cannot be his goals. But I am arguing in this book that they may be more similar to his than many have supposed. It is worthwhile formulating our goals in dialogue with him. If we do so, we cannot formulate them in institutional ways. They must be stated in terms of Christian living. He understood the goal to be the spread of scriptural holiness, about the content of which he was quite clear and specific. In dialogue with him we cannot continue to describe our purposes in vague and platitudinous ways.

It *may* be that in this dialogue we can achieve genuine clarity and conviction about our purposes, purposes that are in continuity with Wesley's. The preceding chapters have proposed some elements of a goal for personal Christian living that develop out of Wesley's own ideas. They are intended to be only suggestive, but what they are intended to suggest is that this may be a fruitful way ahead.

If we could describe the Christian life in a serious way, a way that gave it content and character, we could renew the preaching of the law. For example, if we were collectively convinced that the law of love today calls us to reduce our consumption of resources, and if we thought that through, concretely, in terms of the changed life-style entailed, then we could hold up this demand of the gospel in a way analogous to Wesley's use of the law. If we were collectively convinced that patriarchal dominance is wrong and that children need to be brought up in a nonpatriarchal family context, and if we could see something of what that means concretely, we could state what is required of us by the law of love. Something like this happened in the church through Martin Luther King's leadership of the Civil Rights Movement. We did come collectively to the decision that racism is incompatible with the law of love, and we were able to preach the law, and in some measure implement it, in concrete and realistic ways.

The new issues that agitate us today should not replace the matters on which Wesley preached. Would that we could become as clear as Wesley on what the law of love requires of Christians personally with regard to their ministration to their neighbors' needs or their acquisition and use of possessions! If we could, we would certainly have much law to proclaim!

On issues of motivation also, we would do well to follow Wesley in calling for Christian love. But our account of that love would be informed by the psychological wisdom that has been gained in the past century. That would not mean replacing the Christian call for love with some particular psychological doctrine. The Christian understanding unites the depths of the personal with the utmost reaches of the social as no other teaching does. But the Christian call for love has sometimes inhibited healthy self-affirmation and the open recognition and acceptance of hostile feelings. Also, although faith in our acceptance by God is certainly an important ground for the emergence of Christian love, there is much more to be said. Children need to be surrounded by accepting and affirming love if they are to be able to love others. We cannot simply take Wesley as our guide.

The proclamation of the demands entailed in the law of love, if it is convincing, arouses guilt and the need both for forgiveness and for transformation. Wesley understood that well. It is hard for us, reading him, not to think that he sometimes dwelt too long on the side of guilt. He was convinced that only as one knows deeply and painfully one's need of forgiveness and transformation will one truly appreciate the gift. Perhaps he is right. But guilt can block growth as well as function as a step toward changing direction. We need all the psychological wisdom we can get.

Wesley inherited a tradition that thought of justification and sanctification as occurring once and in that moment resolving the most basic human problem. Wesley worked with that model, although he offers much evidence that matters are not that simple. He changed his mind about when these events occurred in his own life. He recognized that some people fall from grace. He also saw that not every aspect of life comes under the law of Christ at justification. He was particularly distressed that obedience with regard to money was so rare among the regenerate. Ongoing experience in the Wesleyan tradition has provided much additional evidence that conversion in some respects does not guarantee conversion in all. Wesley's reluctant acknowledgment that believers continue to live in sinful ways needs enlargement.

Rather than attempt to fit all our evidence into this traditional mold, we can develop Wesley's doctrine of progressive sanctification yet further. We can define the entry into the Christian life less demandingly. It does involve repentance and justification. But we should agree that we are justified and born again only with respect to those sins for which we have repented. Rare indeed is total repentance, and therefore, rare indeed are total justification and new birth.

The church has often given the impression that every Sunday Christians repent of the same sins, are forgiven for them, and then return to them unchanged the following week. Wesley rejects that understanding. Repentance is too serious a matter to be treated so lightly. To repent is to cease to engage in that sin of which one has repented. Otherwise, it is passing regret rather than *metanoia*. Simply to feel vaguely remorseful and vaguely reassured misses the point for Wesley. His whole focus is on real change.

But the one change whereby one enters the Christian life does not effect all the changes that are needed. Wesley saw that, but his interpretation does not satisfy. He called for a second step that he called entire sanctification. Better would be additional repentance in areas of our lives that were not touched, or at least not adequately affected, by earlier repentance. Like Wesley we may also hope for the weakening of all those motives that are inconsistent with love. But most important, we need, as Wesley so well knew, a progressive Christianization of life, and we need to see this as operating in one area after another, as well as deepening in all.

This analysis suggests that we should think of multiple moments in which we experience *metanoia* and find new life in particular areas. One may be surrendering resentments and defensiveness; another, overcoming racial prejudice; another, breaking out of self-centered existence; another, subordinating sexual appetites to God's larger purposes; another, becoming free of an anti-Jewish way of understanding faith; another, giving up our human-centered vision of reality in favor of a truly theocentric one. The list can go on and on.

But is this just a list of miscellaneous desiderata for the good life? Does it really have anything to do with the Biblical law and gospel? Unless we can answer the latter question affirmatively, this will not be an updating of Wesley, but instead an abandonment of our tradition. The answer can be, indeed, already is, affirmative, but it takes vigorous study and thought to make that evident. Transformations of this sort are required by the law of love and are made possible by that divine power that was incarnate in Jesus. We can show these connections realistically and convincingly. If we do not boldly set out on this project, we are doomed to continuing decline and decay.

But repentance, justification, and sanctification do not exhaust salvation. Our problem is not only sinfulness. We are also broken and oppressed, and we have lost our way. We need to be healed and liberated and to be shown the way. It is true that our brokenness and oppression and lostness are partly the consequence of our sins, but it is equally true that our sins result from our brokenness, our oppression, and our lostness. The New Testament shows that healing the sick, liberating the oppressed, and finding the lost were an integral part of Jesus' work as savior, along with forgiving the sinner. We must reverse the long neglect which these have suffered.

Like repentance, healing, liberation, and finding the way occur in particular areas of our lives, and not, usually, all at once. They *may* accompany release from guilt, but often there are a variety of experiences. Here, too, we must define realistically what we hope for by way of healing, liberation, and finding the way, and identify ways to help people achieve them.

These aspects of salvation may not fit as readily into the life of the church as now structured as those dealing with repentance, faith in God's pardon, and personal transformation in particular respects. They may belong more to small groups and pastoral counseling and social action. But these should be fully rooted in the service of worship.

To some extent, also, these aspects of salvation may belong more to other institutions than to the church. With regard to healing, for example, hospitals and psychological counseling originated largely in the church, and some of this origin is still manifest in what they do. In a pluralistic society it seemed better that some of the ministries initiated in the church be taken over by the state or the public at large. There have been gains and losses. But for the church, when the real healing effected by hospitals and psychotherapists is no longer understood to be part of the salvific work of Christ, then the loss has grown too large. And too often, the secularized institutions that have replaced the Christian ones have lost something of the wholeness that belongs to the healing of the body and the psyche when this is understood to be part of Christ's salvific work. We are making some progress toward reclaiming the connections between all aspects of Christ's salvific work. Much more needs to be done. However important is the healing that occurs in hospitals and professional psychotherapy, the church, if it is to be truly the church, continues to function as a healing community.

Today liberation theologies are convincing to many Wesleyans. For those who are members of the communities that have given rise to them, they often function as a holistic response to the need for a relevant law and gospel truly faithful to Christ. They constitute more or less adequate models of the unity of law and gospel and of the inclusiveness of the gospel that the whole Wesleyan movement needs. But this book is not addressed to those who have recovered the unity of the gospel in this way. It is addressed to those of us who are still floundering. For those who are not members of communities who need liberation from the dominant group, or who do not identify themselves primarily in terms of such membership, simply adopting one or another is not an option. We can learn much from them. But if we proclaim the ideas we have learned from them to others like ourselves, they function as law, effective law in many instances, but they are disconnected from the gospel as we know it.

If we are to make contact with the truths that liberation theologians offer us, we must develop a law that speaks directly to our condition. That law should be informed by our awareness that we participate in oppression of others. It should address first and most directly that in us which supports and undergirds that oppression. If we can be transformed in that respect, then our societal analysis will become more accurate and more authentic. We will cease merely to deplore injustice and oppression in ways that cost us nothing, to ask others to do something about it, and to go on with life as usual. Our transformation will be a part of what needs to happen.

Social action cannot be postponed until we have become appropriately transformed. Wesley believed that Christians should act as the law of love requires even when their motives continue to be mixed. We now need to act for social justice and ecological sustainability even when these seem somewhat disconnected from the limited gospel that actually informs our church. But we also need to work for the authenticity and integrity of the church that can only come as the salvation celebrated in the church becomes inclusive.

There are two further reasons for retaining the social emphasis even as we work on the personal. First, much of what we come to understand about the need for repentance and transformation comes from societal analysis. We would not have understood our personal need to repent of racism if it had not been so clearly shown to us that racism is far more than a personal problem. It has destroyed whole peoples genocidally, and it has psychologically degraded others. It is built into systems of oppression in which we participate. Without this societal awareness, whatever passing racist feelings or occasional racist actions we observe in ourselves could easily appear minor. When we discover that it is just this neglect of our own racism that leads us to tolerate and even support the larger racist structures, then the importance of personal transformation becomes much clearer. We understand that we do, indeed, have much to repent.

Second, we should consider the individual person who repents. Are we as individual as we suppose? Here Wesley is not a good guide. He recognized that sinfulness has a corporate character, but, in part for good reasons, he deemphasized that. He did not see that repentance, faith, reception of God's love, regeneration, and sanctification have a corporate as well as a personal character. Those who are justified and sanctified are not, as he too often implies, autonomous egos. They are who and what they are by virtue of their participation in communities.

Sociological analysis is as important as psychological in understanding the human condition. Purely personal repentance in an unrepentant society rarely changes much. Wesley experienced this with respect to money. Nothing distressed him more than the progressive realization that the Methodists were growing rich! This implied that they were not conforming to evangelical economics. It also meant that all the spiritual problems that beset the rich, making them at best halfhearted in their faith, would beset the Wesleyan movement. In other words, he understood that social conditions have a profound effect on openness to the gospel message.

The actual effect was that Methodists suppressed Wesley's teaching on money. Few were even aware of it, or thought of it as anything more than a curiosity, until liberationists brought it to public attention. Methodism became a conservative supporter of the new industrializing system, even as it provided leadership to the labor movement.

Even when Wesley bemoaned this development and interpreted it sociologically, he may still not have appreciated the full implications. Perhaps it is not possible for any but a few individuals to practice evangelical economics in an economy founded on other principles. At least it seems clear that persistent moral exhortation, even as forceful as Wesley's, has little effect. The realization of this problem had led the Catholic church to distinguish counsels of perfection to be obeyed only by the "religious" from commandments to be obeyed by all. Jesus' economic teaching could then be classed with the former. The Lutheran Two Kingdom doctrine allowed for some separation of the world of business from that of faith. Wesley's evangelical economics influenced his own actions and those of many individual Methodists. But the development of the industrial system forced "realistic" Methodists to enter into its ethos. The early resistance was ineffective and went unnoticed even in the denomination.

An alternative would have been to think through the nature of an economy based on the principle of stewardship. Methodists would then not only have been asked to live that way, but also to challenge the thinking and the structures that were based on the idea that the use of private property was a purely private affair. Could such a challenge have been successful? Would it have been worth trying?

Whether there was anything that Wesley could have done to stem the tide of unbridled capitalism can never be known. The point here is that individual Christians are not simply individual free agents. Who they are, how they think, to what ideas they respond, how they respond, are all deeply influenced by the societies to which they belong. The society both provides and limits the options from among which they choose. Not only is the sinner such by virtue of participation in collective humanity, as Wesley recognized, but also the justified is such by virtue of participating in a society that opens that option. Precisely here lies the importance of the church. Similarly the limits of sanctification, as well as its positive possibilities, are largely set by the nature of society. The brokenhearted are often brokenhearted for social reasons, and prisoners are usually prisoners because of the way society functions. The salvation that Jesus announced and proleptically embodied is the salvation of the world, not of individuals out of that world.

This means that the way personal salvation and social judgment are polarized today is artificial and destructive. Help can come to individuals in a distorted social matrix, but this is limited. The full salvation Jesus proclaimed requires that God's will be done globally. Only as we become collectively more conformed to God's purposes can individuals be truly saved. But, of course, it makes no sense to speak of change in a collectivity that does not involve the individuals who make it up. And there is no likelihood of a positive change in the collectivity until many individuals are first transformed into seekers after the Realm of God, proleptically realizing that Realm in their own lives and communities.

Today there is an additional dimension of salvation that was not so clearly recognized in biblical times. This is the ecological dimension. It is not entirely new, since the Bible does recognize that the fall involved a distortion in the whole created order, not only in the inner life of persons and in human society. Paul does speak of the whole creation longing for liberation. But the knowledge today of how the future habitability of the planet is endangered by current practices, the awareness of the collision between the goal of continuing economic growth and the limited capacity of the natural world to sustain human abuse, the realization that we are wiping out of existence tens of thousands of the species God has created, these are new. Hence when we today speak of the salvation of the world, we can and should give it a fullness of meaning that is only hinted at in scripture.

The forgiveness of sins, the healing of personal brokenness, and liberation from social oppression are all essential ingredients in the fullness of salvation. But if all of that happens, and the natural world continues to decay, that will be a very limited salvation indeed. If famine and disease are decimating the human population, and if our basic stance continues to be one that ignores the causes of these evils, we will hardly be able to claim to have served God's great cause of salvation.

One reason for the emphasis above on lostness is that humanity has so little understanding of what changes are required if God's saving work in the natural world is to have a chance. We are pursuing collectively the wide path that leads to destruction. Nothing can be more urgent than that the Holy Spirit show us the way that leads to life and give us the strength to repent of our now dominant practice of seeking short-term profit at the expense of our children and grandchildren.

Methodism was born when the problems of England were obvious and when John Wesley undertook to respond to them. He rightly saw that the fundamental problem is religious but only because religious transformation involves the transformation of all of life and therefore of society. It is truly ironic that in a time when the problems of the world are even more obvious and critical, and when it is equally clear that the fundamental change that is required is religious, the followers of Wesley are not able to name the challenges they confront, much less undertake to respond to them. A movement born in mission is not able to state its mission realistically and convincingly despite the crying needs which confront it on all sides. Perhaps in dialogue with Wesley we can find our way to serve in our day as he served in his.

CHAPTER 7

Openness to Difference

The Essentials of Christianity

What beliefs should be expected of all United Methodists today? This is a difficult question that the denomination has avoided answering. Instead it has wisely talked about how it expects its members to think theologically and come to their own conclusions. This is the topic of the next chapter. But if we are to live and work together and identify the mission into which we are called by God, we need also to have some shared convictions. Is there a way of coming to the shared convictions we need without formulating a creed or confession that then functions to exclude some who legitimately disagree with its formulations? Can Wesley help us answer this question?

An answer will involve two steps. First, Wesleyans today, as in Wesley's day, are certainly expected to be Christian. Whatever is essential to being Christian is essential to being a Methodist. Second, Wesley had expectations of his own followers that he did not have of all Christians. There was something distinctive about being a Methodist. Does this mean that there are theological requirements on Methodists that go beyond what is essential to Christian belief generally? This first section deals with the first step; the second section will pursue the question of Methodist distinctiveness.

Wesley emphasized the distinction between what is essential in Christianity and "opinions." With regard to opinions Wesley taught that Christians should think and let think, respecting those who held different views. What did Wesley believe to be essential? It can plausibly be argued that Methodists today continue to be bound by whatever Wesley taught to be essential to Christianity.

Jerry L. Walls examines this question thoroughly in *The Problem of Pluralism: Recovering United Methodist Identity*.[1] He provides a thoughtful and insightful examination of Wesley's distinction between essentials and matters of opinion. He then proceeds to argue that followers of Wesley are bound to traditional orthodoxy, accepting all the ecumenical creeds. Indeed, he asserts that these should be adopted as juridical standards for teaching in the United Methodist Church. Freedom of opinion, or at least the right to express opinion, would then be markedly circumscribed.

Since Walls is writing with much the same purpose as I, and since both of us appeal to Wesley in our efforts to establish a basis for unity in United Methodism, it will be useful to examine his argument in more detail. Walls rightly notes that Wesley's examples of opinions on which differences are to be tolerated are generally those matters in dispute among different Christian bodies. He then points out correctly that for Wesley this did not mean indifferentism. Far from it. Doctrines of many sorts are very important to Wesley. Furthermore, as Wesley wrote in "Catholic Spirit": "A man of truly catholic spirit, has not now his religion to seek. He is fixed as the sun in his judgment concerning the main branches of Christian doctrine."[2] Thus far there is no question of Walls's accuracy.

At this point, however, Walls makes moves that I cannot follow. "Clearly," he writes "some doctrines are altogether non-negotiable for 'a man of truly catholic spirit.'"[3] This interpretation is strengthened by what he calls a logical point. To believe one thing is to deny another. Hence, for Wesley to hold one set of beliefs must entail his rejecting others. Walls argues that "anyone who insists on any truth claim at all cannot embrace the principles of pluralism without thereby calling his own truth claim into question."[4] He implies that Wesley's strong beliefs on many subjects made it impossible for him to be tolerant of contradictory beliefs.

Wesley's position is different from Walls's in a way that is quite significant. He agreed that it is very important to think as rigorously and accurately as possible. He had strong convictions for which he argued passionately. He also recognized the validity of the logical point noted by Walls. But one of the convictions deriving from this thinking of which he was most sure was that he, like everyone else, was mistaken in some opinions:

> Although every man necessarily believes that every particular opinion which he holds is true (for to believe any opinion is not true is the same thing as not to hold it) yet can no man be assured that all his own opinions taken together are true. Nay, every thinking man is assured they are not, seeing *humanum est errare et nescire*—to be ignorant of many things, and to mistake in some is the necessary condition of humanity. This therefore, he is sensible,

is his own case. He knows in the general that he is mistaken; although in what particulars he mistakes he does not, perhaps cannot, know.[5]

This point is made earlier in the same sermon from which Walls quotes Wesley's strong polemic against indifferentism. Like Walls, Wesley emphasized that to believe one thing excludes believing other contradictory ones. But he argued against erecting one's opinions into an orthodoxy required of others.

Walls carries his line of argument further when he refers back to the passage quoted earlier. "Traditional theology holds that the main branches of Christian doctrine are 'as fixed as the sun,' (Wesley)." Wesley's statement that the Catholic spirit is by no means a matter of vagueness in doctrine or lack of conviction is transformed into the position that the church has a set of official doctrines that are as fixed as the sun. It then remains only to identify what these are, and Walls proceeds to identify them with the classical creeds understood to be accurate summaries of Biblical teaching.

Wesley did not make these moves. In response to Walls it is important to note that for Wesley faith is not identical with the acceptance of any creed. In fact, Wesley minimized the importance of orthodoxy, which for him involved subscribing to the ecumenical creeds. In "A Plain Account of the People Called Methodists," he wrote that "orthodoxy, or right opinions, is, at best, but a very slender part of religion, if it can be allowed to be any part of it at all."[6] As the preceding chapters have shown, Wesley's deepest concern was for the actual transformation of life. Beliefs were valued according to their contribution to this transformation. As long as it could be shown that a particular belief did not hinder this transformation, Wesley would allow it, even when he disagreed strongly.

It is equally important in understanding Wesley to see that he thought some beliefs were far better than others in accurately describing and encouraging the salvific process. He worked hard to hone his theology accordingly, and he was concerned that his preachers present their message accurately. He could accept believers in predestinationist doctrines in individual cases because these doctrines existed in them alongside the apparent work of the Spirit, but he preached against these doctrines all the same.

The beliefs that he found to be less relevant, and that he had chiefly in mind in his disparaging comments about "orthodoxy," were those that came out of the creeds and out of philosophical theology. Even though he accepted many of them himself and encouraged others to do so, he saw that they were not essential to Christian love. For example, it was profoundly important to him that Christ be experienced as savior and Lord, but he found that this experience was not dependent on traditional statements about Christ's two natures or a particular theory of the atonement. According to Randy Maddox, Wesley believed "that much of the historical debate over Christ's nature was simply unwarranted imposition of philosophical conceptions on the simply-expressed teachings of Scripture and the earliest church."[7]

A particularly interesting test case of Wesley's distinctions among beliefs is found in his sermon, "On the Trinity." He begins his sermon by emphasizing that "religion is not opinion: no, not right opinion, assent to one or to ten thousand truths. . . . Right opinion is as distant from religion as the east is from the west."[8] He demonstrates this by showing that some Roman Catholics are devout Christians despite the many errors contained in their opinions. Even more remarkable to him is that there are Calvinists who are genuine Christians while believing that "the God of love, the wise, just, merciful Father of the spirits of all flesh, has from eternity fixed an absolute, unchangeable, irresistible decree that part of mankind shall be saved, do what they will, and the rest damned, do what they can!"[9]

Still there are some truths very closely connected with vital religion. Among these is the one contained in his text: 1 John 5:7, "There are three that bear record in heaven, The Father, the Word, and the Holy Ghost: and these three are one" (KJV). Having stated strongly that this comes close to the Christian essence, Wesley immediately emphasized the distinction between facts and their explanations. He thought the Athanasian creed the best attempt at explanation, but he denied that explanation is needed or even truly possible. He did not encourage efforts to understand. Further, one is not required to use the language "Trinity" at all, or speak of three Persons, since this is not biblical. Wesley even defended the formulation of Servetus, the hero of the Unitarians, as acceptable.

This might sound as though Wesley simply called for literal acceptance of whatever is said in the Bible, whether or not it makes sense or has importance for Christian life. But the conclusion of the sermon shows that this is not his point. "I know not how anyone can be a Christian believer . . . till God the Holy Ghost witnesses that God the Father has accepted him through the merits of God the Son—and having this witness he honours the Son and the blessed Spirit 'even as he honours the Father.'"[10] For Wesley, the God we encounter in the inward working of the Holy Spirit and in the outward working of Jesus Christ is one and the same as the God whom we know as the Father. To deny this would be to block the path to Christian love.

The beliefs that are required in support of Christian life and experience in addition to the Trinitarian point just made chiefly focus on salvation. It is essential to recognize our profound need for justifying and regenerating grace[11] as well as the actuality and availability of that grace. It is equally important to acknowledge that we are called by God to holiness of life and that grace enables us to grow into that holiness. Failure to accept these beliefs blocks the working of the Holy Spirit within us.[12]

We need a fourfold distinction. First, there is the actual transformative work of God in human life. This is the essence. Second, some teachings about this work support and further it; others block or inhibit it. The latter are forbidden, and instruction in the former is emphasized. Third, there is a body of theology which Wesley saw as very important and on which he had very strong convictions (his opposition to predestination, for example), with regard to which he nevertheless acknowledged that those who disagreed with him could also be authentic believers. And, finally, there are a number of traditional church teachings (on such matters as how the persons of the Trinity are related one to another, for example) to which Wesley personally subscribed but which did not seem to him to make much difference with regard to actual Christian life. Of emphasis on these he often spoke disparagingly, although this certainly did not mean that rejecting traditional formulations was preferable to accepting them.

The Essence of Methodism

The essence of Christianity is the transformative work of the Holy Spirit which Wesley usually expresses in terms of love of God and neighbor, understanding by "neighbor" all human beings. To be a Methodist is, without doubt, to be one who opens oneself to the working of love in the heart by the Holy Spirit. But Wesley believed this was true for all Christians and not for Methodists alone. It does not define the Methodist movement.

To be a part of this movement included requirements that went beyond being authentically Christian. It involved, especially, faithful participation in the Methodist meetings and a willingness to accept the disciplines involved. Did it also require the adoption of particular beliefs not required of all Christians? Are there theological requirements for being Wesleyan that go beyond those for being Christian?[13]

There can be no doubt that Wesley expected his lay preachers to follow his own lead closely. He wanted them to think, but if their thinking took them too far away from his own views, he was far from content. They were to present a united front. When disagreements or uncertainties arose, these were to be worked out at their annual meetings with him, and his word carried. In short, their preaching was to be an extension of his own.

This close control of what the Methodist preachers did was related to the nature of Methodism at the time. Its preachers were not professionally trained or ordained. They were Wesley's helpers in the development of Wesley's movement. One became a Methodist preacher because one wanted to extend Wesley's work. What happened in the movement was Wesley's responsibility. In Wesley's own view and intention, Methodism was not a church, a denomination, or even a sect. Hence this close control over what Methodist preachers then did is not a model for what should happen once Methodism became a denomination.

One way in which Wesley sought to insure that his message would be preached in the movement he had instituted was through the "Model Deed," which contained a clause designed to make certain that those preaching in the new chapels and preaching houses would "preach no doctrine contrary to" that contained in Wesley's *Explanatory Notes upon the New Testament* and the first four volumes of his *Sermons*. This restriction remained in force when legal ownership of the properties passed from Wesley to the British Methodist Conference. Although the restriction of the "Model Deed" has no legal status in American churches, many believe that it should apply to preaching in the United Methodist Church as well.

Would this mean that, however open Christianity as a whole may be to doctrinal differences, United Methodists are bound to Wesley's own position on the issues that distinguished his theology from others? In some sense this is surely the case. What Wesley wanted preached by his followers was what *he* understood to be the gospel. Those who understood the gospel quite differently should preach under other auspices. He recognized their right to do so and respected them. But there was no reason that one who proclaimed predestination, for example, should do so as a Methodist preacher.

Our question now is, How restrictive is this for us? Are we bound to continue to preach Wesley's distinctive doctrines of faith, assurance, and sanctification? Certainly in United Methodism we have not done so. Is the way forward a renewal of Wesley's teaching? Specifically, should we attempt juridically to enforce this kind of preaching?

The previous chapters have suggested one answer. We should engage in dialogue with Wesley on these matters. By ignoring his distinctive emphases we have lost much. On the other hand, his own position did not remain static throughout his life, and it would be impossible to be consistent with everything he said. It would be totally out of keeping with Wesley to repeat particular formulations when these do not correspond either to lived experience or to the best current biblical scholarship. To be faithful to the standard doctrines taught by Wesley involves continuing study of the Bible and attention to the realities of Christian experience in our time.

To follow Wesley's standard doctrines in our preaching is not primarily a matter of dealing with his most controversial and problematic teachings. It is primarily a matter of representing the essentials of the Christian faith as he did, calling always for the love of God and neighbor, and evaluating all doctrines in terms of their relation to this. Even if we were to accept the moral authority of the "Model Deed," this cannot support the credalization of United Methodism.

Insofar as there are specifications of what constitutes Methodist doctrine beyond what is essential to Christians generally, they apply to what is to be preached. Wesley wanted consistency in the preaching, but he did not make detailed agreement a requirement of membership. He wanted as wide a latitude as possible with regard to opinions to be allowed within Methodism. In "The Character of a Methodist" he stated that "the distinguishing marks of a Methodist are not his opinions of any sort. . . . As to all opinions which do not strike at the root of Christianity, we think and let think."[14]

This formulation still leaves unclear what the root of Christianity is. Some might define it as including a considerable range of doctrines, but in his letter "To John Newton" (May 14, 1765), he states that he allows for any opinion which is "compatible with a love to Christ and a work of grace" and explains that the only inquiries he

141

makes of applicants to his societies are these: "Is a man a believer in Jesus Christ, and is his life suitable to his profession?"[15]

John Newton was especially concerned that Wesley excluded those who adopted Calvinist views of particular election and final perseverance. This was because Wesley had described the consequences of these doctrines in harsh terms as inimical to Christian living. Wesley replied that it is enough that Newton held these views to prove that they are not incompatible with love of Christ and a work of grace. In short, the test for membership in a society was not the dangerous implications that Wesley discerned in these doctrines but how they actually worked out in an individual human life. The real requirement for membership was not beliefs at all, but Christian love.

This could be interpreted sentimentally, so that it would have no teeth at all. That would be the danger today. But Wesley did not interpret Christian love sentimentally. For him it was a mode of being that could occur only through the work of the Spirit in repentance and faith. There could be no Christian love that did not express itself in costly works. Only those who showed signs of being and living in this way were accepted.

Today many speak of orthopraxis instead of orthodoxy. This is not enough for Wesley. Orthopraxis might mean works that could occur apart from repentance and faith. For Wesley these are not Christian. Wesley wanted the fruits of the Spirit, not outwardly good actions that are motivated by something other than love. Hence faith was essential for him.

Wesley's definition of the essence of Christianity was not uncontroversial at the time. It is not uncontroversial today. But if the United Methodist Church wants to regain a clear identity, Wesley's distinctions suggest the direction in which that identity could be most appropriately sought. This would require hard work in clarifying how we today understand Christian existence and Christian activity. Would it be possible to come to sufficient clarity that we could present to our membership and to persons who might be interested in joining us a clear picture of our contemporary Wesleyan understanding of the Christian life?

If we could recover and renew Wesley's emphasis on faith, works, and love, modified as appropriate, and could agree that this is the work of the Holy Spirit who can open our eyes to an awareness of the Spirit's work, and to the importance to that work of God's work in Jesus Christ, our account of the Christian life would not be far from Wesley's. This would be especially true if we show how there can be growth in the Christian life as well as falling away, how and why this is so, and how in our fellowship we support one another in working toward fuller love. We could proceed to describe the anticipated fruits of the Spirit and the work we do individually and collectively to express those fruits, especially love.

Today this account would have to be psychologically convincing. It would have to describe what some are actually experiencing and that to which others aspire. We would have to show that what we do together in the church in worship and education and shared action genuinely exemplifies and furthers the account we render of ourselves. We would have to present this whole account in a way that showed awareness of the many and diverse obstacles that block the way to the experience of grace, and the complexities of the public and global problems that impinge on individual life. To follow Wesley in this way would not be an avoidance of theological work—far from it!—but it would channel that work in a particular direction, namely, the direction in which Wesley channelled his. We could work together on clarifying our purposes without having first agreed on any confession or creed. But we would know that theological issues of many sorts would arise as we worked on our clarification of Christian experience and action today.

We would also know that there would be disagreements among us on these theological issues. We would not all agree on which teachings furthered and which impeded the life of Christian love. We would not all agree on how far we could go to allow a place within the denomination for those whose opinions strongly conflict with ours, as Wesley allowed predestinationists in his movement. We would disagree about whether philosophy is useful or harmful in the formulation of our beliefs and, if useful, which philosophy is best to use. We would bring different life experiences as women and men, as old and young, as members of many different ethnic groups from many different cultural backgrounds, that would lead to ranges of disagreement which would have amazed Wesley. And we would differ in our appreciation and appropriation of contemporary biblical scholarship and the historical relativization of past expressions of faith.

But all these disagreements would have for us a different character if we united in our commitment to encourage and embody

Christian love in our life together. We would find some arguments fruitful in promoting this goal, leading to learning from one another and growing in mutual appreciation. The next chapter on the quadrilateral will discuss the norms in terms of which such arguments can be conducted by contemporary Wesleyans.

We would find other arguments useless and even harmful, and we would seek to avoid them. We might understand one who would not set these aside as a heretic in Wesley's sense, that is, one who "obstinately persists in contending about foolish questions, and thereby occasions strifes and animosities, schisms and parties in the church."[16] Heretics in this sense do not belong within the Wesleyan movement, for they do not promote its purposes.

Some questions that Wesley minimized might turn out to be more important for us. For example, Wesley was emphatic that Christian faith depends on the belief *that* Jesus Christ has won our pardon, but he thought that it is not necessary to hold any theory about *how* he has done so. He frequently makes similar points. Often this is a liberating approach.

But when, through the course of changing sensibilities and advancing scholarship, the *that* becomes problematic for many, the issue of exactly *what* is being claimed gains importance. What does it mean that Jesus has won our pardon? To refuse to give some clarification of this assertion is to generate increasing skepticism about it. But any clarification will move in the direction of *how*.

Furthermore, much of importance often follows from the *how*. *How* Jesus saves us affects the question of whether this salvation is effective for those who have never heard of him. Does Jesus' work as savior preclude there being others who have worked salvifically in other religious communities? Does Jesus' salvation have to do only with the forgiveness of sins and healing our sin-diseased souls, or can it have the still wider meaning discussed in Chapters 1 and 6?

Wesley can remain our guide here: we need to press such questions only to the extent that they affect our lives. And we can allow a diversity of answers, testing each against its contribution to the support and strengthening of love of God and neighbor. But we must also ask whether the differences affect the way that love expresses itself in action. Theology of this sort may prove *more* important than Wesley realized.

Religious Pluralism

At the same time that Wesley gave a clear definition to his movement, in terms of life more than doctrine, he also encouraged a spirit of appreciation and cooperation in relation to persons in other communities. He was, therefore, pluralistic not only in his openness to diversities of opinions within the Methodist movement, but also in acknowledging that God worked in other contexts as well, and that this work, too, is to be affirmed and celebrated.

Many of the points made above in explaining Wesley's openness to diverse opinions among Methodists imply also an accepting and affirming attitude toward other Christians. Certainly one would not demand more agreement in opinions with them than among Methodists. Wesley spelled this out emphatically in a sermon on the "Catholic Spirit." Here is his famous text, taken from 2 Kings 10:15, "Is thine heart right, as my heart is with thy heart? . . . If it be, give me thine hand" (KJV).[17]

Wesley, of course, did not derive from this a sentimental notion of mutual appreciation. On the contrary, for one's heart to be right is to love God with all one's mind, heart, soul, and strength and one's neighbor as oneself. It is to have a very particular love for all who share this Christian love. And this love is expressed in action.

He contrasted this shared love with all of those doctrines, forms of church governance, forms of worship, and views of the sacraments, that in fact divided Christians and led to mutual animosities. Each Christian should have strong views on these matters and should participate actively in that particular church which from that point of view is most faithful. But this is no reason to reject fellowship with those who identify with other Christian groups. What is essential is Christian love and that alone.

Wesley primarily had other Protestant groups in mind in this sermon, but what he said applied to Roman Catholics as well. He fully recognized this. He sought to cooperate with Catholics in mutual support just as with other Protestants. In his "Letter to a Roman Catholic," out of his distress over conflicts in Ireland between Catholics and Protestants, he wrote as follows:

> I do not suppose that all the bitterness is on your side. I know there is too much on our side also; so much, that I fear many Protestants (so called) will be angry at me too, for writing to you in this manner; and will say, 'It is showing you too much favour; you

145

deserve no such treatment at our hands.'

But I think you do. I think you deserve the tenderest regard I can show, were it only because the same God hath raised you and me from the dust of the earth, and has made us both capable of loving and enjoying him to eternity; were it only because the Son of God has bought you and me with his own blood. How much more, if you are a person fearing God (as without question many of you are), and studying to have a conscience void of offence toward God and toward man?[18]

After depicting Protestant faith in an irenic way so as to reduce Catholic hostility, Wesley concluded:

In the name, then, and in the strength of God, let us resolve, first, not to hurt one another; to do nothing unkind or unfriendly to each other, nothing which we would not have done to ourselves. Rather let us endeavour after every instance of a kind, friendly and Christian behaviour towards each other.

Let us resolve, secondly, God being our helper, to speak nothing harsh or unkind of each other. The sure way to avoid this is to say all the good we can both of and to one another; in all our conversation, either with or concerning each other, to use only the language of love. . . .

Let us, thirdly, resolve to harbour no unkind thought, no unfriendly temper, towards each other. . . .

Let us, fourthly, endeavour to help each other on in whatever we are agreed leads to the kingdom.[19]

These positions of Wesley were unusual for his time. They are, indeed, still unusual in ours. There is little need here to distinguish between Wesley's own formulations and their relevance for today.

On the other hand, concern for those who disagree religiously has expanded in scope. Relationships with persons of other religious traditions have become far more important than in Wesley's day. Wesley does not provide as much direct help in dealing with this matter as with the others. Nevertheless, even here he is surprisingly relevant.

In his sermon "A Caution Against Bigotry,"[20] he focused on works. His text was Mark 9:38-39, where John asks whether the disciples should stop those not connected with them from casting out devils in Jesus' name. Jesus says: "Forbid them not." Wesley interpreted casting out devils as overcoming the power of evil, wherever and however that may occur. Unlike the sermon on

"Catholic Spirit," this one does not raise the question of the inner motive but focuses on public results.

The text implies that the exorcist is in some way related to Jesus, hence, in application to Wesley's time, a Christian. The issue is whether Christians should support the constructive work of other Christians even if they are in opposing camps or lack proper credentials. As is to be expected, Wesley said they should, and he pressed this to the limits, including Roman Catholics. Indeed, he even included those who were regarded as heretics, such as Arians and Socinians.

Wesley was carried still farther by the logic of his argument. If the work that is done advances God's cause, it does not matter that the actor is not a Christian at all. "Yea, if it could be supposed that I should see a Jew, a deist, or a Turk doing the same thing, were I to forbid him either directly or indirectly I should be no better than a bigot still."[21]

The implication is clear. What binds Christians together in unity is their love of God and neighbor. Wesley connected this indissolubly with the work of Christ. But he did not limit God's working in the world to overcome the power of evil to Christians. God may use others. Christians should be open to seeing that and where this occurs. And when it does happen, Christians are to affirm and support it.

For Wesley this was somewhat hypothetical. For us, it is not. It is obvious that God does much good through secular humanists (our equivalent of deists), through Jews, and through Muslims. Christian ecumenical bodies such as the World Council (and before that the International Missionary Council) have long called for cooperation in good works not only with these groups but with Buddhists, Hindus, and others as well. What were prophetic words in Wesley's day are now commonplaces.

One more point can be made about Wesley in relation to other cultures and religious traditions. He rarely spoke negatively of the others in order to show the greatness of Christianity. This is important. Christians from New Testament times on have disparaged and even vilified Judaism in order to show the newness and salvific importance of Christianity. This was not Wesley's style. His contrast was between authentic Christianity and the inauthentic forms that paraded in its name in the British Isles.

It is true that one of the ways of condemning his fellow Englishmen who had the outward form of godliness without the true religion of the heart was to say they are no better than Jews or Turks. Clearly the assumption here is that Jews and Turks also lack the heartfelt love of God and neighbor that is the reality of the regenerate life. There is little basis for building positive doctrines of Judaism or Islam on Wesley's usual silence and occasional, glancing comments. But it remains the case that Wesley did not build up Christianity by putting down other religious traditions. Indeed, on occasion he could assert the superiority of heathens in comparison with most of those who called themselves Christians. For example, in "Upon Our Lord's Sermon on the Mount, VIII," in discussing the command not to lay up treasures upon earth, he stated:

> With regard to most of the commandments of God, whether relating to the heart or life, the heathens of Africa or America stand much on a level with those that are called Christians. . . . At least the American has not much the advantage. But we cannot affirm this with regard to the command now before us. Here the heathen has far the pre-eminence."[22]

He sometimes affirmed that it would be preferable to "convert the English into honest heathens."[23]

In "A Caution Against Bigotry" there seems to be an exception. In his discussion of casting out demons Wesley made a distinction. Outside of Christendom he noted that crude forms of idolatry persist accompanied by gross immorality. He gave details of vicious practices in Native American tribes near the British colony of Georgia. In such contexts, he thought, the sort of casting out of demons recounted in the New Testament might continue. In contrast, within Christendom, where public morality was not so degraded, the devil must adopt subtler and more sophisticated strategies. Demon possession was a thing of the past. Pride and skepticism were more likely to be the way the devil won his battles.

The picture here of the pagan world is indeed an ugly one, so that Wesley came close to celebrating Christianization as a great advance.[24] The implications for other religious traditions could be very negative. But Wesley did not move in this direction. Immediately after recounting the horrors of pagan life he wrote:

> It were to be wished that none but heathens had practised such gross, palpable works of the devil. But we dare not say so. Even in cruelty and bloodshed, how little have the Christians come behind

them! And not the Spaniards or Portuguese alone, butchering thousands in South America. Not the Dutch only in the East Indies, or the French in North America, following the Spaniards step by step. Our own countrymen, too, have wantoned in blood, and exterminated whole nations: plainly proving thereby what spirit it is that dwells and works in the children of disobedience.[25]

Today we might object that the Europeans were far *ahead* of the Native Americans in cruelty and bloodshed! And we would want to emphasize how much of this destruction was carried on in the name of Christianity. But at least Wesley did not celebrate Christian civilization or use its virtues to justify the conquest of the Americas and the slaughter of their inhabitants. In comparing Christianity with the other great world religions, we could expect him to judge Christians as harshly as any and to acknowledge goodness where he found it.

Although issues about the relation of Christianity to Judaism were far less in the public discussion in Wesley's day than now, Wesley made some valuable suggestions on this topic too. Far from contrasting the Old Testament and the New in terms of their basic understanding of salvation, he emphasized their unity. For example, he argued that Paul did not oppose the covenant given by Moses to the covenant given by Christ. In his sermon on "The Righteousness of Faith," in reference to Romans 10:5-8, Wesley wrote: "It is the covenant of *grace* which God through Christ hath established with men in all ages (as well before, and under, the Jewish dispensation, as since God was manifest in the flesh), which St. Paul here opposes to the covenant of *works*, made with Adam while in paradise."[26] Since Paul associates "Jews" with the covenant of works, Wesley explained that this was true of some Jews just as of many other people. This leaves open the possibility that some Jews, just as some Christians, may live righteously under the covenant of grace.

Randy Maddox has shown that in his later years Wesley went further in his reflections on nonChristians. He explicitly rejected the belief that God could and would save no one apart from explicit faith in Jesus Christ. When preparing Articles of Religion for American Methodists, he deleted Anglican Article XVIII, "Of Obtaining Eternal Salvation Only by the Name of Christ." He could not believe that God condemned to eternal punishment those who had no opportunity to respond to the gospel. In Maddox's words, Wesley taught that "God will judge the heathens with some discrimination after all; not directly in terms of their appropriation or rejection of Christ, but in terms of how they respond to the gracious revelation (light) that they do receive."[27] For example, in his sermon "On Charity," Wesley wrote:

> How it will please God, the Judge of all, to deal with *them* [those to whom the gospel is not preached] we may leave to God himself. But this we know, that he is not the God of the Christians only, but the God of the heathens also; that he is 'rich in mercy to all that call upon him', 'according to the light they have'; and that 'in every nation he that feareth God and worketh righteousness is accepted of him.'[28]

Of course, the gracious revelation received by those to whom the gospel has not been preached is the work of the Holy Spirit that is in fact, in Wesley's view, derived from the atoning work of Christ.

Wesleyans and Religious Pluralism Today

Wesley's few words on other religious traditions do not constitute a "theology of religions" for today. He did not face our situation or raise the questions that press themselves on our attention. In his own situation his views pushed forward the frontiers of toleration, and even support, of those who are different. But transposed directly into our situation, the same doctrines could easily become reactionary. For example, unqualified statements about the necessity of the atoning work of Jesus Christ for salvation seem to imply that other religious traditions have no religiously positive function. To make those statements today, in our much more religiously pluralistic context, would be reactionary.

One possible Wesleyan position is, nevertheless, to emphasize Wesley's statements about the dependence of divine pardon on Jesus' atoning work. One can then drop Wesley's qualifications, including the suggestions that this atonement is from the foundations of the world and hence effective even for those who lived before the time of Jesus and for those who do not know him. One could then argue that apart from conscious faith in Jesus, one cannot be saved. This would draw out the apparent implications of some of Wesley's statements in directions he was unwilling to follow.

A second possible position for Wesleyans is to emphasize the universal availability of forgiveness even to those who do not know of the atoning work of Christ.[29] Those who live by the light they receive are graciously justified. This applies to Jews, from whom we received the teaching of love of God and love of human beings, and among whom such love is to be found. But the fruits of the Spirit can be found in other communities as well. It is the presence of such fruits and not conscious beliefs that testify to salvation.

A third Wesleyan position would be to seek the shared essence of the great religious traditions more openmindedly, instead of assuming that it must be the same as the Christian one. John Hick has made an influential proposal of this sort.[30] He argues that all of the great religious traditions effect in their devoted believers a shift from centeredness on the self to centeredness on what he calls "the Real." In the theistic traditions this is centering on God through love or obedience or surrender. In Hinduism it is overcoming the ego in the discovery that the true self is one with ultimate reality, or Brahman. In Buddhism it occurs through liberation from the illusion of the reality of the self and thus of its separation from other things.

A Wesleyan could agree with Hick that what is truly essential is this transformation or fundamental reorientation. Much of what Wesley said about fellowship and unity with those who loved God and human beings could then be said about those who were thus transformed. Strongly as the Wesleyan would continue to affirm the work of Christ and the Holy Spirit, these, too, would become part of the range of opinions on which difference is possible without breaking fellowship.

While I recognize the validity of all of these moves, none are quite satisfactory to me. I favor a move that may seem a sharper break from Wesley's approach. This fourth Wesleyan approach emphasizes deep differences instead of essential identities. In defense of this as a Wesleyan approach, I begin by noting that Wesley did see Christianity as very different from other religious traditions even if he did not think much about the differences. Had he found this topic important, as it clearly is today, he would probably have studied each tradition openly and honestly to learn what it had to say. It would not have been important to him to find that all the traditions embodied a common essence. My thesis is that students who are not motivated by that quest are likely to be more impressed by the differences.

My second step is to claim that when one studies these traditions openly and honestly with no need to identify a common essence and no disposition to assume that they are without value, one is impressed by the authenticity of the experiences they embody and the

151

wisdom of the insights they have generated. Sometimes Christians who come across these achievements are stimulated to recall similar experience and similar wisdom embodied in their own tradition. They are enabled to revitalize these and gain new appreciation for them. On the other hand, unless they are determined to claim that the Christian tradition contains all worthwhile experience and all wisdom, they are often also impressed that they are encountering something that is new. In short, the fact that these traditions are deeply different from Christianity and from one another does not mean that they are without distinctive value.

A third step is to suggest that although differences sometimes involve contradictions, they do not always do so. Even when there are strict contradictions in the doctrines that give expression or support to diverse experiences and insights, this does not entail that the experiences and insights are themselves contradictory. The Buddhist experience of no-self does not contradict the Christian experience of loving one's neighbor as oneself, even though the teachings suggested by the two experiences are likely to contain such contradictions. If, with Wesley, we distinguish the experience from the associated opinions, we are likely to be able to modify the latter so that they cease to contradict one another without reducing the differences among them.

A fourth step is to propose that the encounter with other religious traditions is an occasion for both teaching and learning. Since our Christian tradition has wisdom that is unique, we should not hold back from proclaiming it. But this does not preclude the possibility that we can gain much of value by listening to the Muslim or the Hindu.

A fifth step is to assert that Christianity from the first has had this character. It has never supposed that the whole of saving truth and wisdom were its possession. The fullness of salvation lies in the hoped-for future rather than in the past or present. Now we see dimly as in a mirror, but then face to face. What we receive from Jesus is the openness to God's Spirit that leads into the fullness of truth. To learn from the Spirit is not to surrender faith in Christ but to embody it ever more deeply.

A sixth step is to affirm that in fact Christians have learned from Stoics and Neo-Platonists and Aristotelians. We have learned from modern science, from historians, from psychologists, and from feminists. Christianity is not true to itself when it tries to display its own strength by defending itself against alien wisdom. Its true strength lies in its weakness, manifest in its openness to learn. It is healthiest and most vital when it boldly appropriates the best that it finds in its world and integrates that with what it has brought from its own past. What is "best" it learns from Christ.

The seventh step, then, is to rejoice that there is now a new range of cultures and religions that can contribute to our understanding. Their history is so different from ours, it expresses itself in ways that are so challenging and so diverse, that the task of learning will take a long time. But as it proceeds we will advance another long step toward that fullness of truth that we can associate only with the eschaton.

This is not Wesley's doctrine. It presupposes a kind of historical consciousness that emerged for the first time in the nineteenth century. And it presupposes a world in which other religious communities are a part of the common experience, a world that emerged only in the twentieth century. A truly Wesleyan doctrine today should take all this into account, just as he was deeply sensitive to the life around him and took into account the best scholarship of his own time. But it is pointless to say that this is what Wesley would do if he were alive today. Wesley would not be Wesley if he were alive today. I recommend it only as one form of a Wesleyan theology of religion appropriate for our time.

CHAPTER 8

The Wesleyan Quadrilateral

Theological Method

The phrase "theological method" is alien to Wesley, as indeed it was to the earlier Reformers, the Medieval scholastics, the church fathers, and, still more emphatically, to the Biblical writers. The term has arisen and become an important focus of debate only as Christians have become perplexed about their relation to the past. It has been especially as critical historical consciousness has distanced us from our basic authority, the Bible, that questions of methodology have come to the fore.

This distancing had begun for some of the intelligentsia by Wesley's day. One reason that Wesley plays so small a role in the typical histories of Western religious thought is that he made no contribution to the new debates of the eighteenth century. These were based on the internalization of what we call the "modern worldview," the view of the world as a great machine. They presupposed that the new science was the normative source of understanding of the world. Whereas prior to the eighteenth century the cutting-edge of thought looked to the past, either classical or Biblical, for wisdom, in the new climate Western thinkers gained confidence in their own ideas, understood them as reason, and believed that reason superseded the authority of the past. The Christian appeal for faith appeared to leading thinkers as an effort to justify an irrational clinging to past authorities.

The question was, then, what authority, if any, ancient documents, and especially the Bible, could still have on rational grounds. Some attributed authority to the Bible only to the extent that it agreed with their own insights. Others believed that it had a supernatural authority which exempted it from the general primacy of reason. But these had to provide rational arguments to justify this supernatural authority.

What we study in intellectual histories tells us very little about what ordinary people, and even most of the intelligentsia, were thinking. We select for study those ideas that were destined to become increasingly influential with the passage of time, not those that seemed most plausible to thoughtful people when first presented. Wesley was an intellectual, aware of and engaged with some of the writings we now study in intellectual history. But he read many of them, not as the emergence of a new cultural age, but as eccentricities to be criticized and set aside. They did not provide the context within which he did theology—only minor conversation partners. His major conversation partners were those whose primary authority was scripture, but who interpreted scripture in ways with which he disagreed. Hence, the major issue for him in the relation of scripture and reason was not how to justify scriptural authority in the courts of reason but how to show the rationality of scripture and to use reason in its interpretation.

This chapter is about the theological formulation that we have come to call "the Wesleyan quadrilateral." This formulation, which first appeared in the 1972 *Book of Discipline of The United Methodist Church* and which recurs in the 1992 *Discipline*, states that the living core of the Christian faith "stands revealed in Scripture, illumined by tradition, vivified in personal and corporate experience, and confirmed by reason."[1]

All four of these norms for United Methodists function differently for us than they did for Wesley. But in the case of scripture, reason, and experience the meanings of the terms are not greatly changed. The greatest difference is with tradition.

Tradition

Today we mean by tradition the whole sweep of Christian life and thought. The Middle Ages are an important part of this tradition. Indeed, the emphasis on tradition has played an important role in healing the ancient animosities between Protestants and Catholics.

With Wesley the situation was very different. Like many members of the Church of England, he appealed to the authority of the early church over against that of later Roman Catholic teaching and practice. His strong affirmation of the teaching and the practice of the Church of England was also in part set over against Roman Catholicism. Thus, for him, the issue was not the authority of the

Christian past in general but which elements in that past had authority over against others. In this regard, next to the Bible he placed the early church and the Church of England, especially the Articles, Homilies, and Prayer Book. In his own words, he was "attached to the Bible, the primitive church, and the Church of England."[2] He was not attached to tradition as a whole.

His attachment to the primitive church and the Church of England was not uncritical. He made his own judgments based on his understanding of scriptural teaching and the experience of his own movement. He appealed to the primitive church against the criticisms of Methodism by the Church of England. On the other hand, he supported Montanists and Donatists against their condemnation in the early church. He felt free to revise the Articles for American Methodism, and he could be somewhat dismissive of the ancient creeds.

Our situation with regard to tradition is quite different. We are open to learning from Roman Catholicism as well as from the primitive church. Luther and Calvin are likely to play a larger role for us than the Anglican Articles, Homilies, and Prayer Book. Above all, when we are struggling to understand and deepen our unity as United Methodists, Wesley's own thought plays a central role.

Is our changed understanding of what constitutes the Christian tradition itself responsible to Wesley? I believe it is. When the General Conference in 1970 declared that the Methodist Articles were no longer to be interpreted in an anti-Catholic way, it was carrying forward Wesley's own spirit of openness to the authentic faith he found among Roman Catholics as described in the preceding chapter. As members of the United Methodist Church and its antecedent bodies had participated in ecumenical discussions about Scripture and tradition, especially with Roman Catholics, and came to new formulations that both could accept, they were surely carrying forward Wesley's own direction. To renew today the exact ways in which Wesley appealed to the authority of tradition would be profoundly unfaithful to him.

Nevertheless, we *can* appreciate and benefit from the general way Wesley used tradition. He read extensively and appreciated much that he read. He learned from what great Christians of the past had experienced, thought, and done. He wanted the Methodists to know this rich resource. But he felt free to make his own judgments about the degree of faithfulness embodied in any past figure or formulation. None had the kind of authority for him that put an end to critical reflection on the matters they treated. Their authority lay in their ability to stimulate and enrich Christian thinking and living. Whatever past figure or writing, creed or confession, tended to hamper Christian thinking and living was to be set aside or criticized.

We may be sure that Wesley wanted his own authority, when he became part of the tradition, to function in the same way. For us, for certain central purposes, he is the most important authority. But that means that we will study his life and thought critically, seeing the ways in which these led to the spread of scriptural holiness. Whatever now impedes that spread is, in faithfulness to him, to be criticized, changed, or set aside.

There is one other feature of Wesley's use of tradition that may have positive relevance for us today. Despite the importance for us to appreciate the whole tradition, including the younger churches and others who have not received an adequate hearing, it may also be important to give special and concentrated attention to the earliest period. We live now in the post-Constantinian era. Increasingly, our churches are disestablished both institutionally and culturally. Wesley did not polemicize against the establishment of the church, but he did see a peculiar purity in the often persecuted church of the earliest period. We also may need to study that period to gain perspective on our own.

To describe the role of tradition as authority either for Wesley or for ourselves as simply an aid in the interpretation of scripture does not fit the facts. Of course, it could and did function for him in that way. But where scripture was silent, tradition, especially the practice of the primitive church was a partially independent guide for later Christians and specifically for the Methodist societies. For us, similarly, the role of Wesley cannot be limited to his guidance in our interpretation of scripture. Despite the great advances in scholarship since his time, his *Notes on the New Testament* and his *Sermons* are still fruitful in this respect. But if we appealed to Wesley only because of this continuing relevance, he would play a small role in our denomination. It is when we face the issue of our distinctive role in the Christian family and our own unity in doctrine and mission that he becomes of central importance for us. We cannot answer these questions apart from examining our origins, and in those origins his thought and practice are largely determinative. We cannot decide what is distinctive about our movement and how its effectiveness can be renewed in a radically changed situation apart from interacting with him.

Embodying the Quadrilateral

This whole book, if it is authentic, should express one way in which the quadrilateral can be embodied. In this case it begins with a particularly important part of the tradition of United Methodism, namely, the thought of John Wesley. But it consciously views that part of the tradition in terms of present experience. It criticizes and hopes to change present experience in view of the tradition, but it also criticizes Wesley in light of present experience.

Wesley was immersed in the Bible as few Wesleyans are today. From him we can learn much about what is truly Biblical and how to relate that to our experience. But Wesley's appeal to the Bible also invites criticism of his theology where it deviates from the Bible. Two centuries of Biblical scholarship require us to engage in such criticism.

In short, a Wesleyan theology for today will draw from Wesley positively but only that which makes sense in terms of current understanding of the Bible and our own living experience. It will discriminate among elements of our own experience those that derive from more accurate understanding of the Bible and new knowledge gained from many sources, on the one hand, and those that express our confusion, our loss of zeal, our new idolatries, and our general sinfulness, on the other. In making these discriminations, it will be informed by the Bible as mediated by Wesley and as understood today on the basis of continuing Biblical scholarship. Unlike Wesley it will recognize that the Bible is a source of some of what is wrong with us, and it will bring critical reflection to bear upon it.

In this book, reason does not stand out as a separate authority. No particular embodiment of reason, such as a particular philosophy or science, is appealed to systematically. However, reason plays an important role. The positive elements in contemporary experience by which it judges Wesley and the Bible are informed by reason. Occasionally the use of philosophy is made explicit, analogous to Wesley's use of Locke and the Aristotelian tradition. And throughout, the intention is to be entirely rational.

This pattern of exemplifying the quadrilateral is by no means the one normative pattern. It is guided by the specific purpose of *this* book, namely, to propose a unifying basis for theology for the United

Methodist Church. This leads to beginning with tradition, and to selecting Wesley from the whole of Christian tradition for special attention. It also focuses attention on the present experience of United Methodists rather than on Christians as a whole. Scripture enters in prominently because of its primacy in Wesley. It enters in also because we United Methodists today acknowledge its authority and are informed by it, and yet are distanced from it as Wesley was not.

The quadrilateral could be equally well illustrated in a book about the message of the Gospel of John for today. There the starting point would be scripture. The elements of the Gospel treated would be selected, at least in part, in terms of the writer's view of the experience of potential readers. The interpretation would be informed by the tradition of Biblical scholarship. The whole would strive to make rational sense. Reason might be appealed to more directly in the form of an approved hermeneutical method.

The use of the quadrilateral can be illustrated also in a doctrinal treatise as, for example, on Christology. The starting point might be either Biblical or traditional. That is, one might begin by an account of the historical Jesus or of the way Jesus was interpreted by Biblical authors, on the one side, or with the creedal controversies or some Christological discussion of later times, on the other side. If it begins with the Bible, it still cannot formulate a doctrine for today without taking some account of the long history that has shaped us. If it begins with tradition it still cannot avoid making some claim about the relation of the tradition to that to which the Bible witnesses. The weighting of these, as well as the starting point, will be influenced by some estimate of how Christ is experienced today. Again, the whole will aim to be rational, and there may be explicit appeal to particular philosophies, forms of historiography, or hermeneutical systems.

All these examples have identified the starting points as either tradition or the Bible. But there is another sense in which the starting point is always experience. My decision to write this book is based on my experience and my judgment about the experience of other United Methodists. My decision to start with Wesley, too, grows out of that experience. The authors of the hypothetical books about John and Christology also begin in this way. This is simply the human condition, and any formulation of theological method that ignores this is inauthentic. Recognizing this fact can lead others to begin by writing about current experience. In particular, women and Christians from non-European cultures, seeing how extensively, and with what little awareness of the distortion involved, theology has been shaped by male European experience, have found it helpful to bring their own experience to the fore. Much of the most authentic theology of our time comes from this new emphasis on the priority of experience.

Beginning with reason is more problematic. However, a Christian may be convinced of the truth of a particular psychology or sociology or philosophy and then consider its implications for faith. If, in the process, scripture, tradition, and experience are treated as mere data to be examined from this point of view, we do not have theology. But if they are respected as additional sources of truth and allowed to interact with the science or philosophy with which the work begins, the result could be responsible theology. Alternately, if the science or philosophy with which one begins is selected *because* of its Christian character, then scripture, tradition, and experience are already in play from the beginning. The result can certainly be a valid form of theology.

Some who agree that there is a diversity of ways in which arguments are conducted and books are written, still want to establish a ranking with respect to authority. For United Methodists, it is said, the Bible is the primary authority, the others are secondary. It can be argued that, whatever the approaches employed, when there is a theological dispute on a central matter of faith, the final appeal is to the Bible. Tradition, experience, and reason may be used in interpreting the Bible, but it is the Biblical position, as discerned in this way, that is decisive.

This view of the ultimacy of the Bible together with the hermeneutical understanding of the quadrilateral appeals to many United Methodists. To others it appears unduly restrictive. Our question now is whether engaging Wesley with this question in mind can help us to move forward to a resolution of this debate or to go beyond it.

Asking these questions of Wesley does not require an exhaustive new study of his views on scripture, tradition, reason, and experience. Fortunately, these have been thoroughly studied by many scholars and are ably reported by Donald A. D. Thorsen in *The Wesleyan Quadrilateral.*[3] Our task is to focus on those features of Wesley's discussion most relevant to our current interests.

The debate within the United Methodist Church came to a focus in the formulation of a new statement on doctrine and doctrinal method for the 1988 General Conference. The 1984 General Conference appointed a commission for this purpose chiefly because of concern that the statement adopted in 1972 failed to provide sufficient basis for doctrinal agreement, especially because it did not adequately emphasize the priority of scripture. In response the Commission proposed that the denomination adopt the hermeneutical model, that is, affirm that the role of tradition, experience, and reason in theology is limited to the interpretation of Scripture.

Other United Methodists believe that the relation between the Bible and reason and experience is more dialectical, that each has a contribution to make that is subject to criticism, correction, and supplementation by the others. Accordingly, they saw the proposed statement as too restrictive. Before adoption by General Conference it was modified extensively to make a place for these people in the denomination. But the basic issue remains unsettled in the actual life of the denomination.

Wesley's authority is claimed for both sides of this debate. Recently, after a careful and extended analysis of Wesley's position, Randy Maddox concludes that the hermeneutical model best expresses his position.[4] He does this despite his criticism elsewhere of imposing on Wesley the Neo-orthodox system which has been chiefly responsible for giving prestige to this model. I believe, on the other hand, that here as elsewhere the imposition of this model on Wesley is a mistake. Since the issue was not posed for him as it is for us, it would be an error to expect a clear and direct answer in his writings. In any case, we would not be bound by his views if such an answer were available. Nevertheless, it is worth posing to Wesley's writings the question that is now clearly formulated for us. The current debate is about the role of reason and experience, and these topics will be discussed in the following sections.

Scripture and Reason

No theologian or preacher has ever been more scriptural than Wesley. A typical paragraph from one of his sermons is full of scriptural quotations. Even the material not placed in quotation marks contains words and phrases from the Bible. Wesley's intention was to preach the message of the Bible.

Wesley grew up immersed in the Bible. He understood himself and other people through eyes shaped by that immersion. For himself he did not have to ask whether the Bible was true as measured by some other standard, because he saw the other standards through Biblical glasses. The primacy of scripture was not so much a doctrine as a reality. This reality determined how he reasoned and what he experienced. It shaped his reading of the tradition. Thus for him there could be no real opposition between scripture, tradition, reason, and experience.

Wesley's strongest statement of the primacy of scripture is in his "Preface" to the *Sermons on Several Occasions*:

> God himself has condescended to teach the way: for this very end he came from heaven. He hath written it down in a book. O give me that book! At any price give me the Book of God! I have it. Here is knowledge enough for me. Let me be *homo unius libri*. Here then I am, far from the busy ways of men. I sit down alone: only God is here. In his presence I open, I read his Book; for this end, to find the way to heaven. Is there a doubt concerning the meaning of what I read? Does anything appear dark or intricate? I lift up my heart to the Father of lights: 'Lord, is it not thy Word, "If any man lack wisdom, let him ask of God."? Thou hast said, "If any be willing to do thy will, he shall know." I am willing to do, let me know, thy will.' I meditate thereon, with all the attention and earnestness of which my mind is capable. If any doubt still remains, I consult those who are experienced in the things of God, and then the writings whereby, being dead, they yet speak.[5]

Formed as he was by the Bible, doctrines *about* Biblical authority were not personally important to him. The Bible has little to say about its own authority. The question of Biblical authority is not a Biblical question. It is a question that arises for those whose basic way of seeing, thinking, and experiencing is not formed by the Bible. They ask how seriously they should take this book, and the answer has to address them in their externality to it.

Since Wesley found the Bible so adequate himself, his basic response to those who questioned its authority was that they should enter into the Biblical world themselves and share his satisfaction in it. When people raised particular objections, he answered them. These objections were chiefly raised in the name of reason. Wesley hardly understood how people could find an opposition between being truly Biblical and being fully rational, since for him no such tension existed. His sense of their unity, almost identity, is powerfully expressed in *An Earnest Appeal to Men of Reason and Religion*:

We join with you then in desiring a religion founded on reason, and every way agreeable thereto. But one question still remains to be asked: What do you mean by 'reason?' I suppose you mean the eternal reason: or the nature of things; the nature of God and the nature of man, with the relations necessarily subsisting between them. Why, this is the very religion *we* preach: a religion evidently founded on, and every way agreeable to, eternal reason, to the essential nature of things. Its foundation stands on the nature of God and the nature of man, together with their mutual relations. And it is every way suitable thereto. To the nature of God, for it begins in knowing him—and where but in the true knowledge of God can you conceive true religion to begin? It goes on in loving him and all mankind—for you cannot but imitate whom you love. It ends in serving him, in doing his will, in obeying him whom we know and love.

It is every way suited to the nature of man, for it begins in man's knowing himself: knowing himself to be what he really is—foolish, vicious, miserable. It goes on to point out the remedy for this, to make him truly wise, virtuous, and happy, as every thinking mind . . . longs to be.

It finishes all by restoring the due relations between God and man, by uniting for ever the tender father and the grateful, obedient son; the great Lord of all and the faithful servant, doing not his own will but the will of him that sent him.[6]

Wesley does not discuss the doctrines that are most likely to be regarded as irrational by his hearers. In another theologian, that might seem duplicitous. But not for Wesley. He has presented the religion of love that is the very heart of his passion. Of course, he accepts the orthodox view of Adam and Eve, of a fall from an original perfection, of incarnation and atonement. But his heart is in the way all this works out in the living experience of loving God and neighbor.

In this passage from the *Appeal* Wesley discusses the relation of his theology to "eternal reason." This is not for him, however, the primary use of "reason," even in that essay. Instead, in "The Case of Reason Impartially Considered," reason is defined as

a faculty of the human soul . . . which exerts itself in three ways: by simple apprehension, by Judgment, and by discourse. *Simple apprehension* is barely conceiving a thing in the mind, the first and most simple act of understanding. *Judgment* is the determining that the things before conceived either agree with or differ from each other. *Discourse* (strictly speaking) is the motion or progress of the mind from one judgment to another.[7]

In this definition of "reason" Wesley stands in the mainstream of the thought of his time. Rex Matthews points out that it corresponds with the first definition in Johnson's *Dictionary*.[8] It also makes good sense today. We apprehend a simple idea, we evaluate it in relation to other ideas, and we employ it in drawing inferences.

Wesley was concerned that reason be given its due and only its due. In "The Case of Reason Impartially Considered" he pointed out to those who undervalued reason its decisive role in all the practical affairs of life, and asserted further that

> least of all are you promoting the cause of God when you are endeavouring to exclude reason out of religion. Unless you willfully shut your eyes, you cannot but see of what service it is both in laying the foundation of true religion, under the guidance of the Spirit of God, and in raising the whole superstructure. You see it directs us in every point of both faith and practice: it guides us with regard to every branch both of inward and outward holiness.[9]

At the same time he addressed a word of caution to those who overvalued reason:

> Let reason do all that reason can: employ it as far as it will go. But at the same time acknowledge it is utterly incapable of giving either faith, hope, or love; and consequently of producing either real virtue or substantial happiness. Expect these from a higher source, even from the Father of the spirits of all flesh. Seek and receive them not as your own acquisition, but as the gift of God.[10]

Wesley's critique of reason, then, was not to limit its role in theology, but to remind us that correct beliefs do not make us Christians. True religion is a matter of the heart, and the enlivening of the heart is a direct work of the Holy Spirit. This in no way conflicts with reason, but it is not encompassed by it.

Wesley did not, in the *Appeal*, follow the widespread custom of those who shared his orthodoxy, of providing arguments for scriptural authority. Unfortunately, he occasionally allowed himself to be drawn into this approach. The result, chiefly to be found in "A Clear and Concise Demonstration of the Divine Inspiration of the Holy Scriptures," is far from satisfactory.

> There are four grand and powerful arguments, which strongly induce us to believe that the Bible must be from God; viz., miracles, prophecies, the goodness of the doctrine, and the moral character

of the penmen. All the miracles flow from divine power; all the prophecies from divine understanding; the goodness of the doctrine, from divine goodness; and the moral character of the penmen from divine holiness.[11]

He supported this kind of reasoning further by presenting the alternatives:

> I beg leave to propose a short, clear, and strong argument to prove the divine inspiration of the holy Scriptures.
> The Bible must be the invention either of good men or angels, bad men or devils, or of God.
> 1. It could not be the invention of good men or angels; for they neither would nor could make a book, and tell lies all the time they were writing it, saying, 'Thus saith the Lord,' when it was their own invention.
> 2. It could not be the invention of bad men or devils; for they would not make a book which commands all duty forbids all sin, and condemns their souls to hell to all eternity.
> 3. Therefore, I draw this conclusion, that the Bible must be given by divine inspiration.[12]

Wesley gives us, thus, two models for relating scripture and reason. The first sprang from his own immersion in the Bible and his conviction that the understanding he had gained therefrom was fully rational. The second was an effort to defend the authority of scripture on alien grounds.

The latter model was typical of the rationalistic orthodoxy of the eighteenth century. It was not expressive of anything distinctive in Wesley's own experience or thought, and, in any case, it is quite useless today. Two centuries of Biblical scholarship and the dominance of the historical consciousness separate us much further from this kind of argumentation than from the Bible itself.

The former model *was* expressive of Wesley's own sense and sensibility, and it is far more attractive to us. We would like to express our Biblically-rooted Christian faith in a way that fulfills the demands of cutting-edge thought. Wesley's example can inspire us to keep trying to find, in this sense, a unity of scripture and reason. This was not easy in Wesley's day. It is much harder today. But it may not be impossible.

Throughout the history of Christianity the question of scripture and reason has focused most frequently on the role of philosophy in theology. Philosophy has played an important role in twentieth-century Wesleyan history, especially through the personalist philosophy of the Boston school. Today process philosophy contends for attention within the United Methodist Church. The issue of the role of philosophy need not arise in the discussion of reason, but it can and often does arise. It arises in part because today many who affirm the role of reason in theology still oppose philosophy. They see the need for reason as embodied in the natural and social sciences and in hermeneutical theory. But they picture philosophy as either dangerous or irrelevant.

The argument against philosophy could be formulated on the basis of Wesley's distinctive doctrine of the spiritual senses, although Wesley did not do this. One could argue that reason based on the physical senses suffices for the range of questions treated in the physical and social sciences so that they can safely be employed by Christians. On the other hand, philosophy, which is also based on the physical senses alone, often deals with issues that can be rightly reasoned about only by those whose spiritual senses are alive.

This criticism can be translated into the terms provided by John Hick and Whitehead's process philosophy. In the former, the issue is whether, as sometimes happens, a philosophy adopts the natural standpoint and approaches the moral and religious spheres reductively. If so, Christians are justified in distrusting it. In the latter, the issue is whether the philosophy limits its data to those given through the senses. If so, again, Christians rightly distrust it.

These replies assume the relativity of philosophies. More strongly than Wesley recognized, we know that what is concluded in the process of reasoning depends on its starting point. We are keenly aware that this starting point is historically and psychologically conditioned. Although there may be some objectivity in the process of judgment and discourse, the outcome depends on what is initially apprehended. To claim authority for any philosophy over theology makes even less sense for us than it would have for Wesley. But this does not mean that theology can safely ignore the issues discussed in philosophy or be unaffected by the conclusions reached. This can be shown in Wesley himself.

For the most part, "reason" in Wesley's use was only implicitly philosophical. It meant simply "the faculty of reasoning," even in the *Appeal*.[13] Philosophy can be understood to be one effort to give expression to this. Wesley believed that, in any case, the Bible does so. Clearly, if those to whom he appealed described the nature of things in a way incompatible with that of the Bible, Wesley would have to argue against the results. Such an argument would have drawn him further into explicit philosophy. Since he thought that the philosophy of his hearers, whether common sense or fully articulated, would not conflict with his Biblical vision, he passed over this possibility.

Actually his vision of reality was quite different from that of the rationalists of his time. They saw God as external to the world, either leaving it alone or acting on it from without. He saw God as energizing all things from within and enlivening all that has life.[14] He did not accent these cosmological matters in his appeal. How conscious he was of this deep philosophical difference is hard to tell. But in fact his vision, derived from the Bible, had philosophical presuppositions and implications of great significance. Wesley's failure to lift them up as such and to challenge the prevailing cosmology in terms of them led to their weakening and near disappearance in the course of Wesleyan theology. They remained as a common note in the Wesleyan doctrine of the Holy Spirit, but without their embeddedness in a total cosmic vision, even this was modified so as to be in less tension with the dominant dualism, individualism, voluntarism, and mechanism. The nineteenth-century movement from free grace to free will expresses this loss.[15]

That Wesley's vision was implicitly philosophical has been noted by others. Mildred Bangs Wynkoop, with whose understanding of Wesley I am in substantial agreement, writes:

> John Wesley's understanding of love can be supported only by an underlying 'metaphysic' which is dynamic in nature. His theological position was not, however, derived from a philosophical point of view. Rather, his religious and biblical insights lead to a metaphysic which . . . commends itself to modern man's new understanding of nature and furnishes a ground for the Christian meaning of life which all men seek, whether or not they know what it is they seek.[16]

Wynkoop sees the work of Daniel Day Williams as developing a theology of love, like Wesley's, but in more explicitly metaphysical dress.[17]

Wesley himself seems to have been hardly conscious that his theology involved a way of seeing relationships, especially between

God and the world, that differed from what the dominant philosophies allowed. He was, however, aware of the epistemological discussions of his time. The long-neglected philosophical side of Wesley's thought has been studied by Richard E. Brantley, in *Locke, Wesley, and the Method of English Romanticism*.[18] Brantley locates Wesley in the cultural history of England and shows that he had a considerable influence in the development of romanticism.

Brantley agrees with other students that the one philosophy by which Wesley was most influenced was empiricism. The most important point was the insistence that there are no innate ideas. Wesley developed his doctrine of faith in response to that empiricism. This is an instance of very considerable influence of philosophy upon him, but he was not passive in simply taking over the philosophy and using it. It led him to employ and develop a particular response. This is the idea that there are forms of perception other than sensory ones, a topic discussed above in the section on faith in Chapter 3.

Rex Matthews has shown that Brantley exaggerates the role of Locke in shaping Wesley's empiricism. Nevertheless, Locke did set the terms for much of the discussion at the time. He did not exclude the possibility of additional senses, but he did not expound it. Wesley could do so without violating Locke's principles. He did so in a way that built a bridge between Locke's philosophy and his own understanding of the teaching of the Bible. Without some such philosophical work on his part, Wesley could not have affirmed the unity of scripture and reason that was so important to him.

The implication for us now is that it is unwise to ignore the influence of philosophy upon our thought or the philosophical implications of our more purely theological ideas. Philosophical ideas are not always derived from the study of philosophy. Although the Bible does not develop philosophical ideas explicitly as such, it depicts a relationship between God and human beings and among human beings that has philosophical implications. It makes sense in terms of some philosophies but not in terms of others. It is a mistake to suppose that Christian faith can be neutral about philosophical issues. It is not necessary for all Wesleyan theologians to reflect about these matters, but for the health of the whole, it is well that some do. Without that, we are not likely to recover the unity of scripture and reason so central to Wesley himself.

Scripture and Experience

Wesley's own experience was deeply informed and shaped by his immersion in scripture. Thus scripture and experience were not for him alien principles. Nevertheless, he was aware of tensions here to a greater extent than between scripture and reason. Donald Thorsen describes the most important instance of this kind. Before Aldersgate,

> Wesley . . . doubted the truth of Scripture, for example, concerning the *instantaneous* nature of conversion by faith. He had not experienced the assurance of a personal conversion and knew of few who had. Although he desired such assurance, he seriously questioned whether he could ever experience it. Peter Böhler and others encouraged Wesley by introducing him to people who had experienced instantaneous conversions. These witnesses, coupled with similar kinds of conversion described in Scripture, led Wesley to a point of belief when he too experienced a sense of personal assurance of salvation.[19]

The importance of this experiential verification of what he already understood to be Biblical teaching can hardly be exaggerated. In fact, it led to teachings that are not clearly in the Bible at all. His account of the difference between "almost Christian" and "altogether Christian" is far more than an exegesis of the Bible. In this case, whether intentionally or not, his own religious experience became a basis for theological doctrine.

The role of experience in informing doctrine can also be seen in his teaching on assurance and entire sanctification. Although he believed that the Bible affirmed both of these doctrines, his teaching went far beyond an interpretation of Biblical texts. Not only his personal experience but also, in these instances, the reports of others affected his teaching. For example, it was the experience of others that led him to the conclusion that some who were justified did not experience assurance and that even those who had experienced entire sanctification could fall.

On the other hand, Wesley more frequently used scripture to critique claims arising from experience. He shared fears about "enthusiasm," and was very skeptical of the value of ecstatic experiences and claims to special revelations. This cannot be seen as purely the influence of scripture, for it was influenced by the rationalistic view that miracles were not to be expected after apostolic times. But he gained from scripture a view of the fruits of the Spirit that depreciated this type of experience.

For Wesley, experience was consistently the ultimate test of scripture. Especially after his Aldersgate experience, he had great confidence that experience would always confirm scripture. This experiential verification was even more important than the coincidence of scripture and reason described in the preceding section. Until such confirmation occurred, scriptural truth remained abstract and even hypothetical. The assurance that comes from experience is the most important role of experience for Wesley.

But the pressure to explain the authority of the Bible from a more objective point of view forced Wesley to develop a doctrine of inspiration. *That* the Bible is inspired by God was a rational claim. How inspiration occurred, what it was, involved reflection about the experience of the authors.

To sustain his high sense of Biblical authority, and to encourage the closest attention to every nuance of the text, Wesley sometimes used language that would satisfy some fundamentalists. In his preface to *Notes on the New Testament* he wrote: "The language of the messengers, also, is exact in the highest degree; for the words which were given them accurately answered the impression made upon their minds. . . ."[20]

On the other hand, the impressions made on their minds seem to be of the same sort as all Christians have through faith, that is, spiritual perceptions. If there is a difference here, it is one of degree. Perhaps the difference is that faith does not provide us with words that are guaranteed to give accurate expression to what is experienced. Wesley may have intended the difference to be at this level. But he also recognized that there are inherent limitations in the ability of language to express the deep things of God.

Since Wesley did not have in view the issues raised in the Fundamentalist-Modernist controversy of the early twentieth century, he was not under pressure to take sides. His reverence for the Bible and his concern that it be viewed as authoritative in detail led to extreme statements on one side. His common sense and honesty led him to recognize the diversity in the modes of composition. Divine direction was needed in a variety of roles, not all well-described by verbal inspiration! For example, in his "Preface to the Book of Joshua" he wrote:

Indeed it is probable they [Joshua to Esther] were collections of the authentic records of the nation, which some of the prophets were divinely directed and assisted to put together. It seems the substance of the several histories was written under divine direction, when the events had just happened, and long after put into the form wherein they stand now, perhaps all by the same hand.[21]

As in the relation of scripture and reason, we confront two basic approaches here. The first tests scripture in experience, confident that its truth will prove itself there. The second uses a theory of experience to explain the truth and accuracy of scripture. Today the first continues to have resonance among Wesleyans. Many remain devoted to the Bible because of its power to challenge, to illuminate, and to heal. The second requires more adjustment to be useful.

The discussion of faith in Chapter 3 showed that there is value in the idea that believers perceive differently from others. They perceive spiritual realities that others do not see. To hold that this was true of those who wrote the Bible makes eminently good sense. But today we would accompany that notion with the emphasis that having eyes opened to dimensions of reality neglected by others does not guarantee inerrancy in the description of those realities. Far from it. Both ignorance and sinful distortion enter into all that believers do and say. There is no reason to exclude the inspired authors of the Bible from this human condition.

Ordering the Authority of Scripture, Reason, and Experience

Clearly for Wesley, and for everyone else, reason and experience operate in other realms beside the close relation to scripture considered so far. Wesley was interested in the science of his day and had no disposition to restrict it or to try to shape it on the grounds of Biblical authority. Indeed, he attributed to it theological importance!

He (God) does not impart to us the knowledge of himself immediately; that is not the plan he has chosen; but he has commanded the heavens and the earth to proclaim his existence, to make him known to us. He has endued us with faculties susceptible of the divine language, and has raised up men who explore their beauties, and become their interpreters.[22]

These men are the physical scientists whom Wesley considers to be "called to a ministry, the same in kind, though different in method, as that of prophets, apostles, and evangelists."[23]

This is not a casual matter for Wesley. He devoted extensive time to the study of scientific writings and summarized what he found so as to make such knowledge available to ordinary people. He did this work continuously over a period of many years. He certainly supposed that knowledge gained from the sciences supplements that gained from the Bible and tradition.

Another essay bears witness in its title to Wesley's sense of the mutually supportive relation of scripture, reason, and experience: *The Doctrine of Original Sin, According to Scripture, Reason, and Experience.*[24] Part I of this essay (pp. 196–238) makes no appeal to scriptural authority except as one source of historical information alongside others. It is a description of historical evidence for universal sinfulness. Part II (pp. 238–314) begins with consideration of several possible explanations, concluding that the one offered in the Bible is the most adequate. There follows detailed debate with Taylor (pp. 240–353), who had argued that original sin is not a Biblical doctrine. Thus the defense of "original sin" begins with general and pervasive human experience, turns on an argument about how it is to be explained, and engages in detailed Biblical exegesis. Although "tradition" does not function as an explicit court of appeal in this essay, it is clear that the idea of original sin comes to Wesley from tradition and that his interpretation of both the facts of history and the Bible are deeply affected by this tradition.

There are few Wesleyans today who would question that when we undertake to interpret the scriptures we are influenced by what we have learned through relatively autonomous reason and experience. We bring questions to the text from ordinary life, and the worldview that informs our interpretation is not derived simply from the Bible. But it is also the case that this relatively autonomous reason and experience are influenced by a perspective shaped by the Bible and Christian tradition.

If the Bible were to be assigned unique authority over reason and experience, this would have to be justified first in the courts of reason and experience. Wesley's own most distinctive vision affirmed all three as mutually confirming, so that this kind of ranking was not needed. But he made concessions to the needs of others, and hence argued extra-Biblically for Biblical authority. There is no escape, in such an argument, from granting prior authority to reason and experience if the Bible is then to be assigned supreme authority for theology.[25]

Finally, most would follow Wesley in allowing some place for reason and/or experience to fill out our teaching on theological issues where the Biblical statements are meager. The more orthodox accept traditional formulations in which this filling out has been prominent and extensive—for example, the classical creeds and a substitutionary doctrine of the atonement. Both liberals and conservatives have doctrines of God which have similarly filled out images derived from the Bible. Hence, in fact, on quite central topics, neither Wesley nor those today who want to give a clear primacy to the authority of scripture, limit reason and experience to a hermeneutical role.

The real issue is whether reason and experience can be employed to criticize and correct scripture as well as to interpret it. If so, our doctrine must arise out of a free interchange among them. This issue did not arise for Wesley in a significant way. It is true that he had doubts about scripture which could be resolved only through personal experience. It is also true that sometimes his interpretations of scripture, such as passages on predestination, may have involved an eisegesis dependent on views of what makes rational sense. But he was genuinely convinced of the fundamental rationality and accuracy of scripture throughout.

During the past two hundred years, however, the issue *has* arisen in a significant way. Wesleyans have played a role in the development of critical Biblical scholarship, which has assumed that many incorrect beliefs—for example about the nature of the universe—were present in the minds of Biblical writers and came to expression in their language. They have shown also that there are conflicting accounts of many events, for example of the Creation, that cannot all be exactly accurate. And, more importantly, they have demonstrated the great variety of theologies in the Biblical text, some of which are not compatible with one another. Reason and experience have played a large role in limiting the features of the Bible that we can now regard as unqualifiedly authoritative.

Contemporary Wesleyans can recognize this and still affirm the supreme authority of scripture for theology. This requires more sophisticated argumentation. But they can regard the separation of the real message of the text from its prescientific cosmology as a part of the hermeneutical role they assign to reason and experience. They can also argue that the determination of the theological import of the

Bible for us must be worked out with criteria internal to the Bible. The task of moving from Bible to theology becomes more complex, they argue, but this is not aided by treating reason and experience as parallel authorities.

Recent decades have shifted criticism to a different level. An important example is with regard to the relation of Christianity to Judaism. The Holocaust and the recognition of Christian complicity have forced reexamination of Christian tradition. What we find is appalling. Most of what Hitler did to the Jews, short of the "final solution," could be justified from Christian writings, including those of Martin Luther.

Obviously, we do not want to continue those traditions. That does not pose a methodological problem. We all agree that at times the tradition must be reformed in light of scripture. But what if we find that the tradition is continuous with scripture? Of course, the Bible does not tell us to put Jews in ghettoes, burn their synagogues, and make their lives miserable. But there are passages in the Christian Bible that do portray Jews as perversely rejecting their own Messiah, as chiefly responsible for the crucifixion of Jesus, and as children of the devil.

Given the new questions we are raising, we must bring to consciousness the profound danger and destructiveness of much that is said in the New Testament in differentiating the new community from the Jewish one. This is the employment of reason and experience in hermeneutics. But when this is done, what next? How do we move from the interpretation of texts, often central ones for Christian faith, to theology? Do we not need to allow reason and experience a positive role at that point too?

Perhaps the clearest example of the problem with maintaining the subordination of reason and experience to scripture is the feminist critique. This critique makes it clear that the Bible is patriarchal through and through. The exceptions, important as they are, do little more than prove the general statement. The tradition, until recently, has only intensified patriarchal dominance.

Contemporary reason and experience have raised the questions which then lead to this interpretation of the Bible. So far there is no challenge to the hermeneutical model. But how do we move from the Bible, so understood, to theology? Do we say that because the Bible is patriarchal, our contemporary Wesleyan theology must be patriarchal also? Or do we affirm that our beliefs today must emerge out of a dialectical interaction between our best current experience and reason, on the one side, and the Bible, on the other?

I am convinced that the latter method points the way ahead. We must show how faithfulness to the biblical tradition itself calls for this. But that is different from setting Biblical authority *over* reason and experience. Women's experience must be given a role in shaping our future thought that was denied to it in the Bible.

Does Wesley support this move? Not directly; but neither does he oppose it. He does not deal with what happens if his synthesis of scripture, reason, and experience collapses. It would be highly uncharacteristic of Wesley to say that in such a case we must stay with scripture however irrational it turned out to be or however opposed to experience. To do that would be to abandon his lifelong commitment to being "a scriptural, rational Christian."[26] It would also require that he abandon his conviction that, in Thorsen's words, "The authority of scripture stemmed more from its existential sufficiency for salvation and holy living than from a theoretic or syllogistic construct for biblical inspiration."[27]

In short, Wesley's own theological method cannot apply when scripture is in conflict with reason and experience. Any formulation under those circumstances must be different from his. But we *can* draw conclusions as to the direction that today is most faithful to his passion for a Christianity that is scriptural, rational, and transformative of life. This would be to seek a new synthesis, a new harmony of scripture, reason, and experience. To do that, we must allow reason and experience free play, even when they criticize scripture. In doing so, we can build on Wesley's vision of God as permeating the world and working redemptively in all human beings. We can draw also on his repeated affirmation of the centrality of love of God and neighbor, responding to the felt love of God for us, and of faith as a perception of God's loving work in us and in the world. We must trust that God's truth will win out. This procedure is closer to Wesley than any other stance we could adopt today.

Postscript

This book is full of suggestions as to what Wesleyans should now do to restore the vitality of our movement and institution. Its proposals are addressed especially to United Methodists. The proposals are, of course, mine, reflecting my judgments and prejudices. No doubt I have interpreted Wesley in terms of these judgments and prejudices. Nevertheless, I would not have made these proposals apart from a fresh encounter with him. I have not merely projected, I have also discovered. I am far more convinced now than when I began to write that we contemporary Wesleyans have much to learn from this remarkable man. I hope that I have presented what I have discovered in Wesley fairly and accurately. I have nothing to gain from misrepresentation or error.

The United Methodist Church will not be able to move forward until it can get beyond the dualities that now divide it: liberal/conservative, evangelical/liberationist, even naturalist/supernaturalist. I think that Wesley can help us here. I believe that my proposals, derived from him, cannot be easily categorized in polarizing ways. I hope that in terms of the deepest concerns reflected in the labels, they are both liberal and conservative, both evangelical and liberationist, both naturalist and supernaturalist. If so, perhaps they are Wesleyan! Wesley devoted himself to a scriptural, rational Christianity. He succeeded remarkably. Perhaps, in interaction with him, that will be a way ahead for us as well.

Of course, I would be pleased if thousands of United Methodists took up my cause along the lines that now appeal to me. But I know that will not happen. My real hope is that more will decide that wrestling with Wesley's thought can help us understand better who we are, how we got this way, and what may be our way ahead. We still have no serious discussion in the United Methodist Church about either our faith or our mission. Perhaps through encountering Wesley anew, such a discussion will begin.

Abbreviations

Wesley's works are cited, whenever possible, in the Bicentennial Edition of *The Works of John Wesley*. If the relevant volumes have not yet been published, then older editions are used. To facilitate the use of multiple editions, I have cited section numbers as given by Wesley in some writings, especially the *Sermons*, and provided dates for letters and for *Journal* entries. References to the *Explanatory Notes Upon the New Testament* are given by book, chapter, and verse.

Journal	*The Journal of the Rev. John Wesley, A.M.*, ed. Nehemiah Curnock, 8 vols. (London: Epworth Press, 1909–16).
Letters	*The Letters of the Rev. John Wesley, A.M.*, ed. John Telford, 8 vols. (London: Epworth Press, 1931).
NT Notes	John Wesley, *Explanatory Notes Upon the New Testament* (London: William Bowyer, 1755; reprint London: Wesleyan-Methodist Book-Room, n.d.).
Works	*The Works of John Wesley*; begun as "The Oxford Edition of The Works of John Wesley" (Oxford: Clarendon Press, 1975–1983); continued as "The Bicentennial Edition of The Works of John Wesley" (Nashville: Abingdon Press, 1984—); 14 of 35 vols. published to date.
Works (J)	*The Works of John Wesley*, ed. Thomas Jackson, 14 vols. (London: Wesleyan Conference Office, 1872; reprint, Grand Rapids, MI: Zondervan, [1958–59]).

Notes

Notes to Preface

1. "Thoughts on Methodism" (1786), §1, *Works (J)* 13:258.
2. See Randy L. Maddox, *Responsible Grace: John Wesley's Practical Theology* (Nashville: Kingswood Books, 1994), 157–58.

Notes to Chapter 1

1. See Max Oelschlaeger, *Caring for Creation: An Ecumenical Approach to the Environmental Crisis* (New Haven: Yale University Press, 1994), 1–18.
2. Harry Emerson Fosdick, *Great Voices of the Reformation: An Anthology* (New York: Random House, 1952).
3. *Journal* 6:63 (May 22, 1775).
4. *Journal* 5:303 (May 5, 1772).
5. *Journal* 5:353 (Feb. 3, 1770).
6. *Journal* 4:157 (April 14, 1756). See W. E. Sangster, *The Path to Perfection: An Examination of John Wesley's Doctrine of Christian Perfection* (London: Epworth Press, 1943, 1984), 104–7.
7. For a careful survey of Wesley's views on classical doctrines see Maddox, *Responsible Grace,* esp. Chapter 4.
8. "The Scripture Way of Salvation," §I.1, *Works* 2:156.
9. "The Way to the Kingdom," §I.10, *Works* 1:223.
10. Ibid., §I.2, 218.
11. *Primitive Physic,* Preface, §8–14, *Works (J)* 14:310–12.
12. John Deschner, *Wesley's Christology* (Dallas: SMU Press, 1960), 185.
13. Theodore Runyon, "Introduction: Wesley and Liberation," in Theodore Runyon, ed., *Sanctification and Liberation: Liberation Theologies in the Light of Wesleyan Tradition* (Nashville: Abingdon Press, 1981), 9–48.
14. Ibid., 46.
15. "Scriptural Christianity," §III.3–4, *Works* 1:170–71.

Notes to Chapter 2

1. *Works (J)* 8:285.
2. "Some Remarks on Mr. Hill's 'Review of all the Doctrines Taught by Mr. John Wesley,'" *Works (J)* 10:392.

3. "Predestination Calmly Considered," §52, *Works (J)* 10:234.

4. "Free Grace," esp. §10–11, 13, 18–20, 23–25, *Works* 3:547–56.

5. "A Thought on Necessity," *Works (J)* 10:480.

6. "On Working Out Our Own Salvation," §III.4, *Works* 3:207.

7. "To John Mason" (Nov 21, 1776), *Letters* 6:239.

8. "Some Remarks on Mr. Hill's 'Review of All the Doctrines Taught by Mr. John Wesley,'" *Works (J)* 10:392.

9. See "From Free Grace to Free Will", Chapter 5 in Robert E. Chiles, *Theological Transition in American Methodism, 1790–1935* (New York: Abingdon Press, 1965).

10. "On Working Out Our Own Salvation," §III.4, *Works* 3:207.

11. "The Repentance of Believers," §I.17, *Works* 1:345.

12. "The Great Privilege of Those that are Born of God," §III.3–4, *Works* 1:442.

13. Lycurgus M. Starkey, Jr., *The Work of the Holy Spirit: A Study in Wesleyan Theology* (New York: Abingdon Press, 1962).

14. "The Witness of Our Own Spirit," §15, *Works* 1:309. Note also the quotation above from "The Great Privilege of those that are Born of God."

15. "A Clear and Concise Demonstration of the Divine Inspiration of the Holy Scriptures," *Works (J)* 11:478–79. The passage is quoted below in Chapter 8.

16. "To John Smith" (June 25, 1746), *Works* 26:199.

17. "To the Revd. William Law" (May 14, 1738), *Works* 25:541–42.

18. "To the Revd. William Law" (May 20, 1738), *Works* 25:546–48.

19. *Works (J)* 14:278.

20. Robert G. Tuttle, *Mysticism in the Wesleyan Tradition* (Grand Rapids, MI: Francis Asbury Press, 1989), 127.

21. Ibid., 151.

22. Martin Schmidt, *John Wesley: A Theological Biography*, 2 vols. in 3, trans. Norman P. Goldhawk and Denis Inman (New York: Abingdon Press, 1962), 1:353.

23. Tuttle, 143.

24. "Upon Our Lord's Sermon on the Mount, III", §I.11, *Works* 1:516–17.

25. "Upon Our Lord's Sermon on the Mount, VI," §III.7, *Works* 1:581.

26. See "Predestination Calmly Considered," *Works (J)* 10:204–59, esp. 232–36.

27. "On Divine Providence," §8, *Works* 2:537–38.

28. "To Dr. Conyers Middleton" (Jan. 4, 1739), §IV.12, *Letters* 2:379.

29. "The New Creation," *Works* 2:500–510.

30. "The General Deliverance," §II.6, *Works* 2:445.

31. Ibid.

32. Ibid., §III.10, 2:449.

33. Maddox, *Responsible Grace*, 68.

34. "The Unity of the Divine Being," §1–6, *Works* 4:61–62.

35. "On Divine Providence," §9, *Works* 2:538.

Notes to Chapter 3

1. "God's Love for Fallen Men," *Works* 2:423–35. The term also appears in the names of Sermons 144, "The Love of God," *Works* 4:331–45, and 149, "On Love," *Works* 4:380–88.

2. *An Earnest Appeal to Men of Reason and Religion*, §2, *Works* 11:45.

3. "A Plain Account of Genuine Christianity," §5, in Albert C. Outler, ed., *John Wesley* (New York: Oxford University Press, 1964), 184.

4. *Works* 7:545–46. The text of the hymn is here quoted exactly as it appeared in *A Collection of Hymns for the Use of the People Called Methodists* (1780). The original second verse was omitted by John Wesley from the *Collection*, and has been restored, with some editorial changes, in subsequent Wesleyan and Methodist hymnbooks.

5. *The United Methodist Hymnal* (Nashville: The United Methodist Publishing House, 1989), No. 384. Ironically, most nonWesleyan denominations have kept the "a" in lowercase.

6. "The Almost Christian," §I.20, *Works* 1:131–41.

7. Ibid., §I.6, 133.

8. Ibid., §I.9, 134.

9. Ibid., §I.10, 136.

10. Ibid., §II.1, 137.

11. Ibid., §II.2, 137–38.

12. Ibid., §II.3, 138.

13. "Upon Our Lord's Sermon on the Mount, V," §IV.10–11, *Works* 1:567–68.

14. Ibid., §IV.11, 568.

15. "The Almost Christian," §I.10, *Works* 1:136.

16. Richard P. Heitzenrater, *The Elusive Mr. Wesley*, 2 vols. (Nashville: Abingdon Press, 1984), 1:102–3.

17. Ibid., 199.

18. "On the Discoveries of Faith," §13, *Works* 4:35.

19. Richard P. Heitzenrater, "Great Expectations," in *Aldersgate Reconsidered*, ed. Randy L. Maddox (Nashville: Kingswood Books, 1990), 165.

20. "The Love of God," §I.6, *Works* 4:334.

21. "On Family Religion," §I.2, *Works* 3:336.

22. "The Love of God," §I.6, *Works* 4:335.

23. *NT Notes*, Luke 15:7.

24. Maddox, *Responsible Grace*, 52.

25. *NT Notes*, John 11:33.

26. For a thorough examination of the development of Wesley's understanding of faith, see Chapter 3 in Rex D. Matthews, "'Reason and Religion Joined': A Study in the Theology of John Wesley" (Th.D. diss., Harvard University, 1986).

27. "The Great Privilege of Those that are Born of God," §I.6–8, *Works* 1:433–35.

28. *An Earnest Appeal*, §32, *Works* 11:56–57.
29. Ibid., §6–8, 46–47.
30. "Justification by Faith," §IV.2, *Works* 1:194.
31. Outler, *John Wesley*, 136.
32. For this account I am indebted to Matthews, "Religion and Reason Joined."
33. *A Survey of the Wisdom of God in the Creation, Or, A Compendium of Natural Philosophy*, third American edition, revised and enlarged (New York: N. Bangs and T. Mason for the Methodist Episcopal Church, 1823), 2:431.
34. Heitzenrater, "Great Expectations," 199.
35. John Hick, *Faith and Knowledge* (Ithaca, NY: Cornell University Press, 1957), Chapter 6.

Notes to Chapter 4

1. "The New Birth," §1, *Works* 2:187.
2. "Natural" here means apart from faith, as Wesley's understanding of faith was explained in Chapter 3. This is not identical with the use of "natural" in the account of John Hick's distinctions.
3. "Original Sin," *Works* 2:172–85.
4. Ibid., §I.4, 175.
5. Ibid.
6. Ibid., §II.9, 180.
7. *The Doctrine of Original Sin, According to Scripture, Reason, and Experience*, Preface, §4, *Works* (J) 9:194.
8. See, in addition to the sermon cited above, his long essay on *The Doctrine of Original Sin* in *Works* (J) 9:192–464. The argument consists in two main elements: the fact of universal corruption, and the Biblical account as its best explanation.
9. See Harald Lindström, *Wesley and Sanctification* (London: Epworth Press, 1950), 41.
10. *Works* (J) 9:316–17.
11. Ibid., 315.
12. "Predestination Calmly Considered," §37, *Works* (J) 10:223.
13. "Letter to John Mason" (Nov. 21, 1776), *Letters*, 6:239–40.
14. "Justification by Faith," §I.8, *Works* 1:186.
15. Ibid., §IV.2, 195.
16. "On Working Out Our Own Salvation," §II.1, *Works* 3:203–4.
17. "The Way to the Kingdom," *Works* 1:218–32.
18. Ibid., §I.7, 221.
19. Ibid., §I.8, 221–22.
20. Ibid., §II.7, 229.
21. Ibid.
22. See "The Scripture Way of Salvation," §III.1–13, *Works* 2:162–67.

23. For a survey of Wesley's occasional speculations on the atonement, see Maddox, *Responsible Grace*, 97–109.

24. My views are spelled out in John B. Cobb, Jr., *Christ in a Pluralistic Age* (Philadelphia: Westminster Press, 1975).

25. "To His Brother Samuel" (April 4, 1739), *Letters* 1:290.

26. "The Witness of the Spirit, II," §V.4, *Works* 1:298.

27. See "The Witness of the Spirit, I," §I.8, *Works* 1:274, and "The Witness of the Spirit, II," §III.5, *Works* 1:289–90.

28. "The Witness of the Spirit, II," §II.3, *Works* 1:287.

29. *Journal* 1:476 (May 24, 1738).

30. "To Richard Thompson" (Feb. 5, 1756), *Letters* 3:161–62.

31. Ibid.

32. "The Witness of the Spirit, I," §I.12, *Works* 1:276.

33. Ibid., §II.11, 283.

34. Heitzenrater provides an illuminating account of the shifts in Wesley's thought in "Great Expectations," 49–91.

35. Maddox, *Responsible Grace*, 129.

Notes to Chapter 5

1. "The New Birth," §II.5, *Works* 2:193–94.

2. Ibid., §II.4, 192.

3. "The Scripture Way of Salvation," §I.2, *Works* 2:156–57.

4. Ibid., §I.6, 159.

5. This oft-repeated but unpublished remark was heard by generations of students in Morris' classes on evangelism at the Candler School of Theology, Emory University.

6. For a helpful account of Wesley's practice and doctrine of baptism, see Chapters 1 and 2 respectively of Gayle Carlton Felton, *This Gift of Water: The Practice and Theology of Baptism Among Methodists in America* (Nashville: Abingdon Press, 1993). The remainder of the book traces the discussion through the intervening period and contributes to the current discussion about baptism in the United Methodist Church.

7. "On Sin in Believers," §I.3, *Works* 1:318.

8. "The First-Fruits of the Spirit," §II.11, *Works* 1:242.

9. Ibid., §II.12, 242.

10. Ibid., §I.3, 236.

11. Ibid., §II.4, 238.

12. §I.11, *Works* 1:341.

13. Ibid., §I.13, 342.

14. Ibid., §I.14, 343.

15. *Works* 7:545–46. See above, Chapter 3, note 4.

16. "The Repentance of Believers," §II.3, 348.

17. "Letter to Sister Bennis" (May 30, 1769), *Letters* 5:138.

18. "Thoughts on Christian Perfection," in Outler, *John Wesley*, 292.

19. "Christian Perfection," §I.8, *Works* 2:104.
20. Ibid., §I.9, 105–6.
21. "Further Thoughts on Christian Perfection," *Works (J)* 11:420.

Notes to Chapter 6

1. "Of Preaching Christ," in Outler, *John Wesley*, 232–37.
2. Ibid., 233.
3. Although I am calling this the "fourth" use of the law, Kenneth Collins has called my attention to the absence in Wesley of the "first" or "political" use.
4. "Of Preaching Christ," in Outler, *John Wesley*, 232.
5. Theodore W. Jennings, Jr., *Good News for the Poor: John Wesley's Evangelical Economics* (Nashville: Abingdon Press, 1990).
6. "The Good Steward," §I.1, *Works* 2:283–84.
7. Ibid., §III.5, 295.
8. Henry Abelove, *The Evangelist of Desire: John Wesley and the Methodists* (Stanford, CA: Stanford University Press, 1990), 9, 17.
9. "The Use of Money," §II.8, *Works* 2:276.
10. *Works (J)* 11:53–59.
11. *Works (J)* 11:59–79.
12. Manfred Marquardt, *John Wesley's Social Ethics: Praxis and Principles*, trans. John E. Steely and W. Stephen Gunter (Nashville: Abingdon Press, 1992), 74.
13. "Of Preaching Christ," in Outler, *John Wesley*, 237.

Notes to Chapter 7

1. Jerry L. Walls, *The Problem of Pluralism: Recovering United Methodist Identity* (Wilmore, KY: Good News Books, 1986).
2. "Catholic Spirit," §III.1, *Works* 2:93.
3. Walls, 63.
4. Ibid., 73.
5. "Catholic Spirit," §I.4, *Works* 2:83–84.
6. "A Plain Account of the People Called Methodists," §I.2, *Works (J)* 8:249.
7. Maddox, *Responsible Grace*, 94–95.
8. "On the Trinity," §1, *Works* 2:374.
9. Ibid., §2, 376.
10. Ibid., §17, 385.
11. This entails the acknowledgment of universal corruption, but here, too, Wesley disclaims knowledge as to *how* this is propagated. See *The Doctrine of Original Sin*, Part III, Section 7, *Works (J)* 9:335.

12. Randy L. Maddox, "Opinion, Religion and 'Catholic Spirit': John Wesley on Theological Integrity," *Asbury Theological Journal* 47 (1992), 76.

13. That there are today formal doctrinal requirements for all United Methodists and especially for preachers is argued in Thomas C. Oden, *Doctrinal Standards in the Wesleyan Tradition* (Grand Rapids, MI: Zondervan Publishing House, 1988). He argues from the history of Methodism in the United States rather than directly from Wesley, although he does show, rightly, that Wesley was far from indifferent to doctrine. He discusses especially Wesley's sermon on "The Catholic Spirit," since he believes it is the one most often used by those who oppose the imposition of doctrinal standards on Wesleyans. He commends Wesley for formulating his doctrinal requirements "not in the form of propositional statements but in candid, simple questions asked from the heart." (97) Beyond the Trinitarian matters noted in the text, examples of these questions are: Is Christ formed in your heart by faith? Have you submitted yourself to God's righteousness which is by faith in Christ Jesus? Is your faith filled with the energy of love? (98) Although Oden draws from this analysis of Wesley support for doctrinal tests with juridical sanctions especially for clergy, and I see Wesley's teaching as supporting a focus on the Christian life as the life of love of God and neighbor, I do not see that we disagree in our interpretation of Wesley himself.

14. "The Character of a Methodist," §1, *Works (J)* 8:340.

15. "To John Newton" (May 14, 1765), *Letters* 4:297.

16. *NT Notes*, Titus 3:10. I am indebted for this reference to Walls, 55.

17. "Catholic Spirit," *Works* 2:81.

18. "Letter to a Roman Catholic," §3–4, *Letters* 3:7–8.

19. Ibid., §17, 13–14.

20. "A Caution Against Bigotry," *Works* 2:63–78.

21. Ibid., §IV.4, 77.

22. "Upon Our Lord's Sermon on the Mount, VIII," §9, *Works* 1:616-17

23. Randy L. Maddox, "Wesley and the Question of Truth or Salvation through Other Religions," *Wesleyan Theological Journal* 27 (1992), 12.

24. That Christianity, and especially Protestantism, has had *some* positive effect on public morality is argued in *The Doctrine of Original Sin, Aaccording to Scripture, Reason, and Experience, Works (J)* 9:192–464.

25. "A Caution Against Bigotry," §10, *Works* 2:67.

26. "The Righteousness of Faith," §1, *Works* 1:202–3.

27. Maddox, "Wesley and the Question of Truth," 18.

28. "On Charity," §II.3, *Works* 3:296. Maddox, "Wesley and the Question of Truth," 18, cites also "Large Minutes," Q. 77, *Works (J)* 8:337; and *NT Notes*, Acts 17:28.

29. Something like this is suggested by S. Wesley Ariarajah, "Evangelism and Wesley's Catholicity of Grace," in M. Douglas Meeks, ed., *The Future of Methodist Theological Traditions* (Nashville: Abingdon Press, 1985), 138–49.

30. His most definitive formulation is in Part Four of his Gifford Lectures: *An Interpretation of Religion: Human Responses to the Transcendent* (Houdsmills, Basingstoke, Hampshire, GB: Macmillan Press, 1989).

Notes to Chapter 8

1. *The Book of Discipline of The United Methodist Church, 1992* (Nashville: The United Methodist Publishing House, 1992), 50 (¶66); see the parallel formulation, 76 (¶68).

2. "Farther Thoughts on Separation from the Church," §1–2, *Works* (J) 13:272–74. For this quotation and for much of this discussion I am indebted to Ted A. Campbell, *John Wesley and Christian Antiquity: Religious Vision and Cultural Change* (Nashville: Kingswood Books, 1991, Chapter 6.)

3. Donald A. D. Thorsen, *The Wesleyan Quadrilateral: Scripture, Tradition, Reason & Experience as a Model of Evangelical Theology* (Grand Rapids, MI: Zondervan Publishing House, 1990). A more recent study is that of Maddox, *Responsible Grace*, 36–47. See also the detailed discussions of scripture in Scott J. Jones, *John Wesley's Conception and Use of Scripture* (Nashville: Kingswood Books, forthcoming 1995); of tradition in Campbell, *John Wesley and Christian Antiquity*; and of reason and experience in Matthews, "Reason and Religion Joined."

4. Maddox, *Responsible Grace*, 46.

5. "Preface to *Sermons on Several Occasions*," §5, *Works* 1:105–6.

6. *An Earnest Appeal*, §28–9, *Works* 11:55.

7. "The Case of Reason Impartially Considered," §I.2, *Works* 2:590.

8. Matthews, 137.

9. "The Case of Reason Impartially Considered," §II.10, *Works* 2:599.

10. Ibid., §II.10, 600.

11. *Works* (J) 11:484.

12. Ibid.

13. See *An Earnest Appeal*, §30ff, *Works* 11:55ff.

14. See Chapter 1 above. See also *The Doctrine of Original Sin*, Part III, Section 7, *Works* (J) 9:336.

15. See Chiles, Chapter 5.

16. Mildred Bangs Wynkoop, *A Theology of Love* (Kansas City, MO: Beacon Hill Press, 1972), 11.

17. Ibid. See Daniel Day Williams, *The Spirit and the Forms of Love* (New York: Harper & Row, 1968).

18. Richard E. Brantley, *Locke, Wesley, and the Method of English Romanticism* (Gainesville: University of Florida Press, 1984).

19. Thorsen, 130–31.

20. *NT Notes*, Preface, §12.

21. *Explanatory Notes Upon the Old Testament* (Bristol: William Pine, 1765), 1:701.

22. *A Survey of the Wisdom of God in the Creation*, 2:339.

23. Frank W. Collier, *John Wesley Among the Scientists* (New York: Abingdon Press, 1928), 84–85.

24. *Works (J)* 9:196–464.

25. This point is also made by Walls, 81ff., in his argument for the primacy of scriptural authority.

26. "Letter to Freeborn Garrettson" (January 24, 1789), in Outler, *John Wesley*, 85. Outler comments in a note on p. 84 that this letter, written at the age of eighty-six, "serves as an occasion for Wesley to reaffirm yet once again his lifelong ideal: 'a scriptural, rational Christian'."

27. Thorsen, 77.

Index

191